now or never

The term 'quantum activist' is trademarked, which I did not know when I used it. For information on quantum activism, please reference the work of Dr. Amit Goswami, who originated the term. I have now revised this manuscript and removed all references to the term in future hard copy and Kindle versions.

now or never

a visionary map
for quantum activists

will wilkinson

now or never © Natural Wisdom LLC, 2016

First Edition, 2016
Second Edition, 2018
Natural Wisdom Press, Ashland, Oregon
www.willtwilkinson.com

ISBN-13: 978-1540608932

ISBN-10: 154060893X

Printed in the United States of America

"In *Now or Never*, Will Wilkinson has forged a radical toolkit for reconnecting with the sacred self, Earth, and all living beings. He has proven that there is no 'business as usual' to return to and also provided a map for Sacred Activists to navigate the uncharted terrain of both the inner and outer worlds. The journey is terrifying, beautiful, and oh so worth the effort, and this book is required reading for making it."

- **Carolyn Baker, Ph.D**, author
Collapsing Consciously: Transformative Truths for Turbulent Times
and *Return to Joy with Andrew Harvey*

"What does it mean to be human? What is our place in the cosmos? What will our future be? In tackling these ancient questions with a new voice, *Now or Never* provides guideposts for the courageous reader willing to walk a path lined with the twin sides of the "crisis" coin: danger and opportunity."

– **Guy R. McPherson**, Professor Emeritus
of Conservation Biology, University of Arizona

"It's refreshing to discover an author who cares passionately about the world and who looks to the natural order for innovative solutions to global problems. *Now or Never* urges readers to discover and reference the intelligence apparent in the myriad and synergistic relationships beyond ourselves. Bravo for this encouragement to look up and out, to remember what we've forgotten, and for reminding us that we all belong to a bigger life."

– **Laura Sewall**, educator, conservationist,
author, *Sight and Sensibility*

"*Now or Never* presents a virtual tool kit for blending spirituality, nature, and social activism. Integrating these new habits enables the reader to enjoy what Will calls The Transformational Lifestyle. His applications and stories about their proven effectiveness with clients give me hope that we might actually navigate our evolutionary crisis toward a promising future, should enough of us take personal responsibility for playing our unique part in the adventure."

– **Master Charles Cannon**, Founder
Synchronicity Foundation for Modern Spirituality.

"I have known Will for 40 years and have always thought of him as the quintessential 'renaissance man.' *Now or Never* is his magnum opus and it combines his empowering and innovative thinking with stories from his remarkable life of learning. Written in a down-to-earth voice, Will inspires us to wake up, grow up, and show up in the world as agents of change at this perilous but exhilarating moment in human history."

– **Suzanne Anderson MA**, Co-author, *The Way of the Mysterial Woman: Upgrading How You Live, Love and Lead*

"In this time of great emergency, Will Wilkinson is just what we need – an emergent seer. His wise and playful book, *Now or Never*, helps us emerge from our all-too-convenient hiding places and see that now is the time to give our unique gifts – because it is too late to do it sooner."

– **Steve Bhaerman** aka Swami Beyondananda
Humorist and author, *Spontaneous Evolution* (with Bruce Lipton)

"In these times of so much information and so many choices it is a welcome relief to have the clarity Will Wilkinson provides in *Now or Never*. As one who has had to recreate my life from scratch, I found much insightful guidance from this inspiring yet practical manual for living life to the fullest - 'on purpose' as Will so aptly puts it - so that we maximize our potential, opening doors to new aspects of ourselves."

– **Kia Scherr**, Co-founder, One Life Alliance.

"As a seeker for several decades on how to reclaim my innate instincts and 'stay awake,' I have read many books. Will Wilkinson's *Now or Never* is currently my Hall of Fame discourse on these subjects. His style of writing made me feel as if I was sitting next to him eagerly asking, "Tell me more!" This book is one that you absolutely want to have on your nightstand."

– **Steve Sisgold**, author of *Whole Body Intelligence*

"Will helped me on a writing project years ago and it's great to see him coming out with his own book, *Now or Never*, that presents so many of the amazing experiences he's had in his life in a way that helps us learn lessons about our own lives. What a book!"

– **Yakov Smirnoff,** comedian,
Professor of Love and Laughter at Missouri State University

the quantum activist:

knowledge: *every thought, word, feeling, and action generates a ripple effect in human consciousness.*

commitment: *being the change we wish to see in the world.*

focus: *obsession with one impossible goal.*

You are here for a reason,
here on earth and here on this page.

You need what we all need:
hope that these are not the last,
fleeting decades for a failed species,
but a transformational opportunity,
that depends on what I do, on what you do,
on who we be.

We yearn to know that we can make a difference,
that it's not too late for us to change direction,
to help heal the world and create a future
where our great grandchildren can thrive.

We can do this. Will we?

It's now or never,
here on this third planet from the sun
we call home.

ҩ

What if ?

dedication

Since the first edition of this book was released near the end of 2016, many readers, colleagues, friends, and clients have contributed to the evolved insights you'll find in this revised manuscript.

Particularly, the term "quantum activist" has emerged from the ether to premiere here. Former readers will notice how the plethora of processes featured in version one have focused into the seven practices you'll find here. Much appreciation to everyone who contributed to these improvements, especially our book club members.

Thank you Tashina, my beloved partner, for your honest, tough and tender love. You've inspired and balanced me, and made me laugh almost every day for 24 years. To my business partner Christopher, thank you for your grounded friendship. And big thanks to Geoff and Linda in Auckland for your loving, generous support.

I'm grateful to my grandfather, Abdul Hadi Nasser al-Din, for your deathbed quantum transmission. I abide still in that moment with you.

Thank you to the old Russian ship captain who rescued a 21-year-old hippie – me – from a possible detour to Siberia. Your intervention taught me that truth can transcend culture and that God is a trickster who sends unlikely allies to save the day, just in the nick of time. Perhaps that's what we need now.

Finally, I dedicate this book to our spiritual teacher, Yogi the Cat, who just left this dimension and whose lingering, sweet love will forever be a life changing, transformational gift.

To everyone with the courage to embrace their personal Now or Never moment and follow through, this book is for you.

Will Wilkinson
February 24, 2018 in Auckland, New Zealand
and May 1, 2018 in Ashland Oregon

visionary map

foreword by andrew harvey

I am delighted and honored to write this brief foreword to Will Wilkinson's terrific and elegant new book, *Now or Never*. Will brings a unique mix of erudition, humor, passion, and profoundly schooled intelligence to bear on what is the most essential problem of our time: how to face our escalating, catastrophic global crises without becoming overwhelmed and paralyzed.

Will calls his book *Now or Never* because, unlike the popular majority of our modern spiritual teachers, he is unafraid to address the tremendously painful and challenging evolutionary crisis we find ourselves in and to chart a bold course of action. However, he also understands that there can be no relief from debilitating fear, despair, and heartbreak without reaching deep within our most visionary selves. Will illuminates in poetic and inspiring fashion just how transformed our lives may become when we act from passion and compassion to bring about the depth of radical transformation we long for, personally and globally.

This path calls for enormous courage, plus a profound hunger in one's sacred imagination to see our world already transformed and healed, even as we face the darkness and difficulty that could doom our best efforts, were we to forget or fail to hold fast to those hopeful visions.

Fusing rigorous down-to-earth realism with the higher realism of sacred imagination — complete with its purest, wildest, and holiest intentions — is most certainly the key to acting effectively from a place of joy and energy and hope, even in profoundly frustrating conditions.

But *Now or Never* proposes much more than a new kind of visioneering rooted in ancient spiritual traditions. Will also invites us to ground our visions by committing to a specific date: May 1, 2025. His intention is to inspire us to author our own grand humanitarian initiatives and stream them together towards what he's calling a New World Party, and to begin celebrating our success right now. I find his highly inventive process of starting in the future and working backwards revolutionary!

I also agree that we *must* start now, supporting each other to launch our own bold, wild, audacious projects, however improbable they may initially seem. I love Will's confidence and unflinching courage to dream the impossible... and then set about to make it happen, step by dedicated step! The extremity of our situation here in the twenty-first century calls for nothing less ... which might seem insane. But Divine Love has always seemed insane to those who do not know and cannot bear its power. The time is now or never to embody the insanity of Divine Love and infuse it within wonderfully grand plans such as Will is daring to propose.

To fully embody the insanity of Divine Love we must devote ourselves passionately to daily practices that sustain our connection with both the Divine and the *embodied* Divine, which is nature. We need the strength of nature, the vital force that flows in everything that lives, as well as the wisdom that emerges from our connection to transcendence. We're offered a menu of accepted traditional spiritual practices plus quirky, wonderfully eccentric practices that Will has created and refined with clients and organizations over many years.

Will calls the context for our explorations the "Wonder Field" and many readers will recognize the work of author/researchers like Lynne McTaggert and Gregg Braden. I was fascinated to read the many dazzling discoveries about plant intelligence and the extraordinary mental and even psychic capacities of animals. This recalls the great shamanic traditions and reminds us to be humble, grateful, and nakedly ecstatic in those relationships, to continually bathe in the luminous energies of our Mother.

One aspect of Will's book that I find most encouraging is his exhortation that authentic sacred activism requires maintaining a balance between an inner life filled with authentic mystical experience and commitment to radical, urgent, wise action in the world: Too much inner life, and we become junkies of mystical sensation and orgiastic magical thinking; too much outer action and we become burned out fanatics. The life of a sacred activist will always be a volatile dance of dynamic opposites, a marriage of ruthless realism with child-like amazement.

Welcome dear readers to this wild dance of *Now or Never*, where we can learn how to fully show up in this devastating and amazing time with our whole selves pledged to the greatest possible adventure, to midwife the birthing of a new humanity to populate a new world.

> – Andrew Harvey
> Author of *The Hope, A Guide to Sacred Activism*

If you find that your heart has hardened,
one of the gifts you should give yourself
is the gift of the inner wellspring.

You should invite this inner fountain to free itself.
You can work on yourself in order to unsilt this,
so that gradually the nourishing waters begin
in a lovely osmosis to infuse and pervade
the hardened clay of your heart.

Then the miracle of love happens within you.

- John O'Donohue

welcome

Something wonderful is happening.

That's how the first edition of this book also began. I've used these four words countless times and now believe they cast the best opening spell for a learning adventure like this.

Something is beating your heart, my heart, every heart, while simultaneously steering a billion stars. Makes you wonder, doesn't it?

You'll find plenty to wonder about as you read. For starters, what does the title mean? Yes, it's an old Elvis Presley song, but it's also my best attempt at describing the pivotal moment we find ourselves in.

Now ... we quit strategies that have failed to solve our problems (personal and global) and learn / master a radically new approach (quantum activism),

or

Never ... we keep trying only harder and eventually accept our fate as yet another doomed species, while binge watching with nachos.

You may be approaching your own Now or Never moment, eager to disprove the lie that you are powerless and incapable of doing anything significant to contribute, ready and poised to get trained up for the adventure of your lifetime.

If you keep on reading we'll know that you are.

I began revisions for this second edition in New Zealand, fresh from a weekend Now or Never workshop where we initiated our international network. We extend our welcome to you now, to become a fully activated quantum activist.

First, we need to find out exactly what that means.

෨

When you get to a place
where you understand
that love and belonging, your worthiness,
is a birthright
and not something you have to earn,
anything is possible.

- Brené Brown

i n t r o d u c t i o n

What is a quantum activist?

A quantum activist understands that their every thought, feeling, word, and action generates a ripple effect throughout the field of consciousness, unlimited by space and time. He/she is committed to focusing their energy towards positive change in world. They are obsessed with achieving one impossible goal, from the inside out.

1. Knowledge   2. Commitment   3. Action

You may have never heard the term before. I hadn't until it floated out of the ether one evening during a brainstorm with my wife. "Quantum" - the smallest possible discrete unit of energy or matter. "Activist" - a person who campaigns to bring about political or social change.

I describe a quantum activist as any person who directs their smallest discrete units of energy to catalyze political or social or spiritual change.

While there's no age limit for quantum activists, my experience is that almost all of us, plus those who want to learn, are over 50. I'm always thrilled when I meet someone younger who shows an interest and aptitude, but it's rare. Of course, a tidal wave of young quantum activists could work miracles and revolutionize what we're doing. So, welcome!

what can one person do?

That's the question millions of us ask as we survey the global landscape. Any sort of personal initiative, like voting, signing a petition, attending a rally, donating to a good cause, driving a Prius or – on the inner side of the equation – praying, meditating, and visualizing, all seem about as effective as peeing in the ocean.

We ask the same question about our personal lives. What can we do about financial debt, illness, trouble in our marriage, kids out of control, the weird neighbor, the boss, the investors, the lack of meaning, and most of all, the escalating stress that has turned so many lives into a wearying struggle interrupted by peak moments of fleeting enjoyment?

We're asking the wrong question.

More important than *what* we can do is *who* we are. This book invites you to trade "What can one person do?" for "Who can one person be?"

who are you ?

When you look up at the stars on a clear night, do you feel small or large?

It's easy to feel small... you're looking at something vaster than you can compute. But think of a bowl with a marble in it. Which is bigger? The bowl, obviously, because it contains the marble.

So, returning to you and the stars, which seems bigger now? Are you the bowl (your awareness of the starry sky) or are you the marble (your body and ego)? If you identify as a separate human then you're the marble, you're small, and the bowl is the vast starry sky. This makes it inevitable to become discouraged when you ask, "What can one person do?"

But if you identify with the awareness that contains the vastness of the visible cosmos, then you are large. You are the bowl that holds the marble. You are consciousness itself and consciousness contains everything. The moment you identify as consciousness, rather than just as a separate individual, you *become* that vastness.

This transformation of identity opens a door to actualizing your potential for exerting extraordinary impact. Conscious within consciousness, you can influence the entire matrix of our numberless universes in this very moment. The same principle that says "you cannot disturb a flower without troubling a star" means that every breath and thought impacts... everything. As it always has. As it always is in every moment.

"Who can one person be?" Someone conscious within the consciousness that contains everything. Suddenly, you don't feel so small and ineffective, right? "What can (this) one person do?"

You can become what I call a quantum activist, broadcasting who you are through everything you do to impact consciousness. Example: wash a dish with love and inspire forgiveness in strangers 3,000 miles away.

Try on this empowered, non-local identity the next time you and the stars come out to play together. Perhaps you'll feel that shift from "What can one person do?" to "Who can one person be?"

the quantum effect

Millions of people are familiar with The Observer Effect, which states that the act of observing influences what is being observed. Millions more of us know about the power of prayer and the "hundredth monkey" phenomenon. These are all examples of quantum activism.

The guiding principle: how we express ourselves (thoughts, words, feelings, and actions) *always* has an impact. The proposition to prove: when we focus intention together it's possible to trigger change in others at a distance, without needing direct physical contact or education.

A friend of mine participated in a now famous meditation experiment in Washington, DC in 1993. Between 800 and 4,000 TM practitioners meditated in the city over a two month period with the stated intention of lowering the crime rate. As reported online: "A week or so after the start of the study, violent crime (HRA crime: Homicides, rapes and aggravated assaults, measured by FBI Uniform Crime Statistics) began decreasing and continued to drop until the end of the experiment.

"Before the project the researchers had publicly predicted that the coherence group would reduce the trend of crime by 20%. This prediction had been ridiculed by the Chief of Police who asserted that the only thing that would decrease crime that much would be 20 inches of snow. In the end, the maximum decrease was 23.3% below the time series prediction for that period of the year.

"This significant reversal in the predicted crime trend occurred when the size of the group was at its largest in the final week of the project and during a blistering heat wave." [1]

Reports like this explode the doubt that someone like you or me — not holding public office, not having millions of dollars, and not being a rich celebrity with 25 million likes on Facebook — could make much of a difference. Imagine, meditating together to lower crime rates. What else might we accomplish by focusing our intentions at the quantum level?

Weekend meditators could never have transmitted enough energy to achieve that result in DC. Focusing conscious intention to produce results in the physical world is what quantum activists are able to do. Anyone can learn how and you will as you read.

break down precedes break through

How does one become a quantum activist?

It usually takes something dramatic and painful to disrupt life and trigger a heroes journey of initiation towards some kind of victory and mastery. The road to becoming a masterful quantum activist begins in the heart. Here's how mine began.

I am a 20-year-old college student in Canada and the Kent State shootings are happening right now. I stand in shock, staring at our small black and white TV as students my age sprawl on the ground, bleeding and dying. I feel my breath catching; I'm trembling, and tears pour freely.

For the first time in my life I feel unsafe. I begin to shrink.

Later, reading a Newsweek article entitled "My God! They're Killing Us," I make a snap decision and jump on a ship for Australia. My plan? To get as far away from the madness as possible.

I sail for Australia... but I come back.

timothy leary's mistake

I was 16 when Timothy Leary said, "Tune in, turn on, and drop out." I followed his instructions. Millions of us did. The result? We left society to be run by others. Unfortunately, many of those others turned out to be self-serving sociopaths. Here in the twenty-first century I believe that many baby boomers are re-examining our decision to drop out.

We wonder, "What might society have become if we'd tuned in, turned on, and *engaged?*"

What if we'd gotten *more* involved back then by taking a stand *inside* the system: running for public office, starting good companies, learning how to be responsible citizens, and speaking truth to power as part of the mainstream, rather than from outside in our many side streams? Thank you, everyone who hung in there and contributed as best you could.

I didn't. I started meditating, was introduced to God by LSD, and joined a spiritual community with hopes of regaining a measure of my security, gutted by the horror of Kent State.

the problem with the counter culture

Millions of us dropped out. Some joined communes and stayed like I did (for 21 years). Others drifted aimlessly from one meaningless job to another. We gave up hope in a system we knew was deeply corrupted. We became part of the "counter culture," which some say began with John F. Kennedy's assassination in 1963 and stretched to 1974 when Nixon resigned, according to some historians.

Many of us got married, had kids, bought station wagons and cared about mileage. We lived those New Riders of the Purple Sage lyrics: "The people who live round the bend in the river have forgotten their dreams and they've cut off their hair."

Either we left the mainstream to assume a contrary position or we dove into the mainstream and forgot our dreams. Some of us have been "in opposition to" ever since; others have been silent enablers of systemic madness. Today our society is more dysfunctional than ever. So, do we pat ourselves on the back? "We were right, ahead of our time." Or do we feel guilty? "I sold out!"

reaching our 'now or never moment'

Who knows if dropping out was right or wrong. Who cares, really? That question can only lead to judgment and shame, or to denial and even more apathy. If necessary, let's take a breath, forgive ourselves, and appreciate that those decades off-line were not totally wasted. We learned a lot and now is the time to put what we learned into practice. I'm sixty-seven as of this writing. I should be retiring, right? But who can retire in our world on fire?

We should be embarrassed. Look at the world we're leaving our grandkids. Golf, three times a week, really? That's an appropriate response to the grim state of the world, with our signatures all over it?

I've seen a sign in stores: "You break it, you buy it." We broke the world. We've got to own that. We've also got to fix it. No energy for that? What are we going to do instead — drink protein shakes and rail at elected officials and evil CEO's until we die, hiding from the guilt and shame of leaving such a colossal mess for our grandchildren to clean up? BTW, we told our kids to clean up their rooms, didn't we? How about we clean up the world? Here's a thought: Maybe we could do that together. And maybe it will take more than recycling.

History is well populated by heroes and tales of their mighty deeds. But the stories we love most are about ordinary people who reach a point where they *must* take a stand. They may put it off as long as possible, until the pressure builds to a breaking point. Suddenly, the choice they've been avoiding becomes the choice they must make *now*. A profound shift occurs in one climactic moment when they finally choose to act.

It's what I call their "now or never moment."

We love that moment in films. Here is that exact same moment in your life and mine. It's now or never for me, for you too if you're reading this book. Did you think it was just curiosity that drew you here, partner?

Your desire to help, your hunger for fairness, your frustration with the system, your passion for doing good, and your nagging sense that something entirely different is needed and possible ... *this* has brought you to these pages. This is the invitation, arising from within you, to take the road truly less traveled and become a quantum activist.

They say a film that's good for eighty minutes but sucks at the end will be remembered as a lousy film, whereas one that sucks early but has a great ending will be remembered as a good film.

The way we finish our lives matters. It's not over until it's over. It's not too late to change the script, to write in a happy ending, but this is not editing, it's a rewrite of how the human story ends. We're exposed to an unrelenting onslaught of dystopian programming every day, particularly in the torrent of sci-fi films that present inevitable future wastelands. Elon Musk warns that Artificial Intelligence (AI) poses the greatest danger to human survival but his solution is to colonize Mars, while failing to understand that we would just take the virus with us, in us.

Robots are fundamentally disconnected from the organic web of life.

They represent the perfect crowning creation of disconnected humans, proudly building silicon replacements to survive in a toxic, burning world that is increasingly unfit for oxygen breathing, carbon based life forms. Disconnected humans can't survive and won't survive. Attempting to do so is a waste of time when we don't have time.

The new story line? Transform ... or else. It's now or never.

the rise of quantum activists

There are no celebrities in nature. Trees don't compete against each other for headlines and awards. Alpha animals don't train to become champions of their forest. Insects don't vote for their next Great Leader. The desire to be visibly great is distinctly human. It's called "narcissism" and it's fundamentally contrary to the way nature works. 99.9999% of us are not and will never be super stars. But we *can* become quantum activists, transformed humans fully interconnected in an organic predecessor to the Internet that some call "the innernet."

There's an indigenous principle: "Anyone can be chief, except someone who wants to be chief." Our world is run by those who *really* want to be chief. They have big egos. They want power and control.

Quantum activists don't crave power or glory or money. We contribute. We serve. We cooperate with each other and understand that humans are only as unique and intelligent as every other species, each in our own wonderful way. We ponder an intriguing question: "What might we accomplish together?" and we leave out no one.

Found online: "One biologist has been working on a simple language, the first to allow "two-way communication between humans and wild animals, *Wired* reports. Divers showed dolphins how to press on a keyboard to get items they wanted, and the dolphins showed interest, even bringing friends along. Communication worked best when humans first established a rapport with the dolphins, imitating them and making eye contact as humans do with each other." [2]

You'll be reading inspiring stories about nature and species intelligence like this as we go along, describing the kind of respectful interaction humans can begin to develop with other species. It starts with humility. Other species know plenty that we don't. In fact, the stories and studies I distribute throughout the book will blow your mind.

Humans *are* uniquely unique. We alone wield the power to destroy other species. Sadly, that's exactly what we are already doing and at a record rate. Meanwhile, they keep us alive every time we eat – *if* we're eating them, rather than the junk we make from chemicals. And, we can learn something vitally necessary from them about effective quantum activism.

For instance, starlings flock together in massive numbers. This phenomenon is called "murmuration." From the Woodland Trust Nature Detectives: "A murmuration of more than six million starlings was recorded in 1999/2000 at Shapwick Heath National Nature Reserve in Somerset... each starling follows the movement of the six birds flying closest beside it. And because they have lightning-fast reactions – under 100 milliseconds – and superb spatial awareness, if one bird changes speed or direction, those around it do too. This ripples through the murmuration and means that they're able to fly at speeds of around 20mph without crashing in mid-air." [3]

What amazing coordination, synchronization, collaboration. Imagine if we could develop that skill. Birds do it by aligning with the six birds closest to them. What if we started paying attention to our immediate environment, to those we're with, and learned how to thrive together? That sounds like a different sort of leadership paradigm.

Quantum activists don't follow any leader; we fly together. We respect chemistry and the alchemical potential in every relationship.

"call me trim tab"

Buckminster Fuller was thirty-two when his only daughter died. Blaming himself for not being home when she passed, he waded out into Lake Superior to commit suicide. A thought interrupted him: what if his life could become an experiment to see what one little person can do? He chose to find out and is now revered as one of the greatest inventors and thinkers of the twentieth century. He introduced the trim tab metaphor to explain how a small number of people can make a big difference. [4]

The trim tab turns the rudder which turns the ship. Bucky said, "Call me trim tab!" He's got a lot of company these days; enthused change makers all over the world. This book champions their efforts and reveals how quantum activists can steer the ship of humanity in a better direction.

As Margaret Mead said, "Never doubt that a small group of thoughtful, committed citizens can change the world. Indeed, it is the only thing that ever has." Hence, the potential for quantum activists, most of whom will likely remain virtually invisible, yet participate on the "team."

looking ahead while looking back

If you Google "human near-term extinction," you'll find scores of sites presenting everything from hysterical raves to scorn. Some writers offer sober studies with statistical evidence to prove we're committing species suicide. Some conclude that we could be the dumbest species on the planet because no other species fouls their own nest the way we do.

The road to hell is paved with good intentions. Bravo to those who are doing their best but sorry, it's not really working and we're running out of time. Struggling to solve problems, without changing the thinking that created those problems, just creates *more* problems. Trying to right the wrongs of the past keeps us imprisoned in trauma. But traveling into the future and focusing intention backwards ... who's tried that? It's only possible from the quantum field.

Join us. Become a quantum activist. Let's change the future *from* the future, by learning how to ripple together in that limitless dimension beyond space and time.

seven quantum practices

1. Love: "*Something wonderful is happening.*"

2. Connection: "*I am nature.*"

3. Imagination: "*What if?*"

4. Balance: "*And.*"

5. Vision: "*Say it, see it, feel it.*"

6. Navigation: "Heal the past, create the future, enjoy the present."

7. Transmission: "*I am, I see, I feel, I will.*"

Central to all seven practices – which are explained in detail in the chapters ahead – is the wisdom woven into this poetic instruction from my first mentor, which still rings true today:

"Let love radiate, without concern for results."

These words are spells. They are formulated to change things, to change you. You are small and insignificant ... you are vast and magnificent. That depth of change can happen in an instant, as your eye travels from word to word and the meaning between the lines ignites something already alive in you. It's a quantum moment, described in *A Course in Miracles* as The Holy Instant.

We experience what we express. When we are experiencing The Holy Instant, it becomes instantly available for others to share. That's called entrainment, an osmosis-like process we shall soon explore.

Whatever transformation we personally experience broadcasts far and wide, instantly reaching those who are resonating with us at that moment in the unfolding history of our universe, a history that is wholly written in this one, present, quantum moment of emerging reality.

Consciousness changes.
Behaviors change.
We get different results.
We create a different future.

This is what one person can do.

࿇

Mount the stallion of love and do not fear the path—
Love's stallion knows the way exactly.
With one leap, Love's horse will carry you home
However black with obstacles the way may be.

~ Rumi

part one - tune in

love

What we want we do not have,
what we have we do not want,
who we are is what we need.

Love is my word for God. Love includes emotion and romance but I capitalize the word to differentiate between aspects of love and Love itself, which contains and animates every thing and being, including us.

Life is subjective and none of us translates Love the same way. We've been taught that we all live in the same objective reality but quantum research is disproving that concept. As already mentioned, The Observer Effect is a theory stating that simply observing a situation or phenomenon necessarily changes that phenomenon.

How we look changes what we see. Quantum activists look through the eyes of Love. Our core principle is:

"I am an aspect of Love expressing itself
and my expression has an effect on everything and everyone."

When any person accepts this identity, they are immediately freed from confusion about who they are. You are Love, a unique, one-of-a-kind frequency of Love, creating a personal reality in synergistic collaboration with all of life. This means that you are enough.

Who you are has *always* been enough. You don't need a separate God or praise or success or material wealth to have value. You belong, you have a place in this world, you are needed, and you are valued. I'm speaking about the *truth* of you, beyond your human personality. This identity will become more familiar as you travel these pages. It is not blasphemous to claim this identity; it is blasphemous to deny it and claim to be something separate from Love, separate from God.

"I think, therefore I am," becomes "I am, therefore I love."

Knowing this, even theoretically at this point, demands that we accept full responsibility for ourselves in order to address personal and global problems from a fundamentally different vantage point. The question, "What would God do?" becomes "What would I do?" Since God is Love, expressing hatred and exacting punishment is not an option. Those strategies belong to the God of religious belief.

Being Love is merely a controversial theory for those who are not actually experiencing Love as their primary identity. If you're not, you can. Reading with an open heart and mind will call in this experience for you.

the world is in our hands

Our world is on fire. Everywhere we look we see threats to human survival: Record heat, rising oceans, infectious diseases, fermenting racism, suicide attacks, political insanity, murmuring panic in financial circles, deceitful leadership obscuring the threat of socially accepted horrors like unproven GMO foods, fracking that pollutes ground water and incites tremors, and toxic vaccines that doom our children to indentured servitude in a system that bills us to get sick and then bills us to get well enough to finance savage surgeries and petroleum based medicines that keep us sick until we die in pain and confusion.

But we are blind to the obvious in a thousand ways. Here's one example. Visit the American Cancer Society website to read their annual report (which reads like a report from any other corporation with products and services to sell), complete with numbers about this epidemic that struck 1.7 million and claimed 600,000 lives in the US in 2016. [1]

"In the US, one in two women and one in three men will develop cancer in their lifetime. Now, a similar rate has been reported in the UK, with a new study published in the *British Journal of Cancer* claiming one in two men and women will be diagnosed with the disease at some point in their lives." [2]

Imagine if you read that five jumbo jets crashed today, killing all on board. Then it happened again tomorrow, and the next day, and every day. This is how the math works on cancer deaths right now. But, since it doesn't make headlines, we remain blind to the horror.

If you object to my earlier examples of all that is woefully amiss with our corrupt and deceitful society, for instance if you insist without proof that all vaccines are safe, that GMO foods are a boon to mankind, that fracking is totally harmless, and that chemotherapy is a gift from God, at least acknowledge the fact of this cancer epidemic. If you have a family of four, statistics say that two of you will likely contract cancer.

That's not a conspiracy theory, it's a modern statistic.

It's doubtful that visitors to the American Cancer Society website are aware of the irony – and insanity – of their name: The American Cancer Society. It must rank as one of the most successful organizations in the United States. It has succeeded wildly. We now *have* a cancer society.

Nor would visitors likely be aware of this statement: "Cancer, above all other diseases, has countless secondary causes. But, even for cancer, there is only one prime cause. Summarized in a few words, the prime cause of cancer is the replacement of the respiration of oxygen in normal body cells by a fermentation of sugar." [3]

Doctors do know something about the relationship between sugar and cancer. "We can detect cancer using the same sugar content found in half a standard sized chocolate bar. Our research reveals a useful and cost-effective method for imaging cancers using MRI." [4]

How many doctors tell their cancer patients to stop eating refined sugar? You get Jell-O in the hospital. Most doctors are uneducated about "the one prime cause" of cancer, definitively proven by the German physiologist, medical doctor, and Nobel laureate (nominated forty-seven times and winning in 1931 for his research on cancer), Dr. Otto Warburg who I quoted above.

Or, doctors *do* know about this but have chosen to ignore it.

moving on

One innovative way to face hard truths is through imagery, which we'll be employing throughout this book. Rumi's words from the opening quote echo across the centuries and present evocative symbols. "Mount the stallion of love and do not fear the path..." Consider the imagery of this verse and zero in on two significant elements: the stallion and you.

What might the stallion represent? I believe that this is the force we are riding, the same force that - as I said before - beats our hearts and steers the stars. In other words, we needn't rely on our own power; we can ride. "Love's stallion knows the way exactly." Thank God; we don't have to figure everything out.

Who are you in this scenario? You are the rider. But you are not steering. "With one leap, Love's horse will carry you home." Urgent as our situation on Spaceship Earth surely is, this verse champions a very different kind of "activism." What you do only becomes important when you know that Love is what you are and Love charts your course.

tune in ... turn on ... engage

As my friend Andrew Harvey wrote in his generous foreword, "... unlike the popular majority of our modern spiritual teachers, (Will) is unafraid to address the tremendously painful and challenging evolutionary crisis we find ourselves in and to chart a course of action."

I'm a life-long meditator who off-ramped the "spiritual bypass" many years ago and got informed about what's happening in our world on fire. I have friends who don't watch the news because it's too negative. I get that. Well, find better sources of news. Apathy breeds inaction and too many smart, caring people have dropped out. If we truly care about a livable future for our great grandchildren, we must jettison ourselves from the comfort bubble we've been sleep walking in for decades and acclimatize ourselves to life here in the real world of urgent challenges.

Four stages of human potential:

1. Those who don't know and don't know that they don't know.

2. Those who don't know and *know* that they don't know.

3. Those who *know* but don't know that they know.

4. Those who know and *know* that they know.

Leave those in category one alone. No one appreciates being roused when they're sound asleep. Category two people have begun to stir in their dreams. Shine your light to beckon them from bed. Category three folks are ready to learn. When the student is ready, the teacher appears.

That's been me for much of my life. That's who most of you readers are. My best teachers have always confirmed that I already knew what I needed to know... They helped me remember. I'm telling you the same thing in this book.

Category four are teachers. We know and we *know* that we know. What do we know? As Socrates's said: "I know one thing: that I know nothing."

Such is the mindset we begin with: beginner's mind. Yes, I have wisdom to share, gathered throughout a lifetime of learning and teaching. But you have wisdom too and the fact that you're reading means you're ready to access and actualize more of your own. My words can help catalyze your memory of what you already know.

Quantum activists are born, not made, but potential needs actualizing.

If you are resonating with these words and compelled to read on, you could be a quantum activist in the making. But you won't find me trying to convince you about anything. Those of us called to contribute this way are an odd breed. We are sensitive in ways foreign to most people.

That can make it difficult to even be here. I've always felt like a stranger in a strange land. I've always lived on the outskirts of town, never feeling like I totally fit in. But I've come to appreciate my uniqueness, which makes it easier to appreciate what's unique about others.

So, we begin with Love. We focus on who we can be, not what we can do. Quantum activists function in a fundamentally different way, contributing from the inside out.

This means that we don't do what we do just to heal or improve or enrich ourselves. We act to express Love, in whatever ways are most appropriate. Learning how to do that is the subject of this book.

about the practices

Each practice has seven elements: name, purpose, spell, movement, feeling, image, and the form of the practice itself. This will seem complex and is, initially, but even a minimum amount of repetition quickly turns complexity into simplicity, as all seven discrete elements begin to merge together into one momentary experience of quantum activism.

Name and purpose are self explanatory, the others deserve comment.

Each practice is cued by a spell, a handful of words carefully combined to carry a specific energetic signature. Like all spells, they can create magic. Repeated often enough, they change your programming, developing new neural pathways to enable thinking differently.

Movement is about how the energy of this practice moves. Through experimentation, each one has revealed a unique pattern of quantum activity. I can't guarantee they will all be the same for you; my description is meant to help you discern and experience for yourself.

A feeling is assigned to every practice and, again, they will be unique for everyone. Emotion is the key element. Until we deeply feel something, it remains theoretical. In time and with enough practice, you will come to experience each practice as a distinct feeling state.

Every practice also comes with its own image, drawn from nature or human invention. You'll notice that these images show up throughout the manuscript, mentioned in various contexts.

Finally, the practice itself is a physical activity that you undertake while thinking and feeling as explained. Ultimately, all these elements will anchor together in the name of the practice so that using the name will immediately evoke its purpose, spell, movement, feeling, and image as you perform the practice, eventually in just a few seconds of linear time.

You may have found my imaginative invitation to become a quantum activist appealing. I hope so. If you are serious about developing the kind of mastery I've begun to describe, your apprenticeship begins with this first practice. I urge you to begin now with Practice One and add in each new one as they are presented.

practice one - love

"Something wonderful is happening."

Love comes first.

When we use this spell to connect with Divine wisdom and organic synergy, we create a sane context for everything that follows. Something wonderful *is* happening, everywhere.

When we forget and plunge forward in the problem / solution paradigm we are trying to solve problems with the same thinking that created them. Einstein defined insanity as doing the same thing and expecting different results.

Starting with Love is different thinking.

The image for this practice is sunrise. The sun rises without our help. Imagine shoveling darkness all night and assuming we finally got it all out of our room when the sun rises. That would be insane. The sun rises on its own and is rising somewhere on the planet in every moment.

The movement in this practice is a flow down from above and up from below, connecting "heaven and earth," merging our sense of the Divine with our experience of the material world.

The practice itself is a three-phase breathing process:

1. Inhale, feeling gratitude for the gift of life.
2. Pause to feel the grace of being alive.
3. Exhale generosity with your out breath.

Declare the spell silently: *"Something wonderful is happening,"* as you breathe slowly in and out, pausing in between, and focusing the feelings of gratitude, grace, and generosity.

In time, this practice will anchor firmly to the word "Love" and just hearing it or saying it or thinking it will cue the spell and the full experience of this quantum practice in action will unfold.

Yes: I am a dreamer.
For a dreamer is one who can only find his way by moonlight,
and his punishment is that he sees the dawn
before the rest of the world.

~ Oscar Wilde

what if?

*May I be like
One of those small children
Who, with one hand,
Hold on to their father,
And, with the other,
Pick strawberries and blackberries
Along the hedges.*

~ Francis De Sales

What if?

Those two words open magical doors. We can ride them to ... anywhere. Imaginary leaps were natural for us as children, not so much as adults.

We don't use these words as often as we could, if we hope to imagine our way out of the predicament our lack of imagination has created.

This chapter invites us to begin our exploration of The Wonder Field — my name for consciousness — a deliberately playful term meant to remind us of the eternal value of child-like thinking.

Before we can develop an understanding of The Wonder Field, we first need to examine what has suppressed our innate abilities to imagine and create. In the film, *The Matrix*, Morpheus referred to this as "the world that has been pulled over our eyes." True. We grope our way through a blinding maze of deception. Asking "what if?" shines a light.

seeing the obvious

"*The Emperor's New Clothes* is a short tale by Hans Christian Andersen about two weavers who promise an emperor a new suit of clothes that is invisible to those who are unfit for their positions, stupid, or incompetent. When the Emperor parades before his subjects in his new clothes, no one dares to say that they don't see any suit of clothes until a child cries out, 'But he isn't wearing anything at all!' " [1]

This well-known story is a relevant parable for the twenty-first century where we have perfected denial to an art form. Here's just one example:

> Waste at the Pentagon is nothing new. But recent revelations suggest that it may be reaching historic levels. "The Special Inspector General for Afghan Reconstruction has uncovered scandal after scandal involving U.S. aid to that country, including the creation of private villas for a small number of personnel working for a Pentagon economic development initiative and a series of costly facilities that were never or barely used. An analysis by ProPublica puts the price tag for wasteful and misguided expenditures in Afghanistan at 17 billion, a figure that is higher than the GDP of eighty nations. [2]

For intrepid readers genuinely interested in this example of sanctioned insanity, I suggest you Google "Abram tanks." Talk about an emperor with no clothes! There are scores of examples like this: climate change deniers, lobbyists whitewashing the potential dangers of fracking, GMO foods, excessive vaccines, etc., etc., etc.

These and other issues are modern versions of that ancient parable. The deceit is obvious. Where's a kid with a strong voice when you need one?

change starts at home

The idea of being part of the trim tab and helping to steer humanity in a better direction may be an appealing idea, but participating means actually *being part of the trim tab*. That requires starting right where we are with the circumstances and people closest to us.

That's easy, once we regain the sense of wonder we were born with. We arrived fully connected, plugged in, integrated within the web of life. We didn't even need toys at first ... just being alive was enough. All of us have memories — maybe just faint recollections now – but I've never met anyone who wasn't in touch with childhood magic.

I am ten, standing under the street lamp in front of our house, watching snowflakes fall. I've dropped my hockey equipment bag to the icy ground and am gazing upwards. Snowflakes land on my face and melt.

A car crunches by, the driver slowing to see what this kid is looking at. A dog barks. Our front door opens. "Billy?"

Mother scolds me for "standing there like the village idiot."

I warm up at the kitchen table, sipping hot chocolate and silently replaying the epiphany of moments before. "The top of my head is the highest point on earth exactly here, with the space above connecting me to a billion stars.

Wow!"

This is more than a memory; it's a threshold moment branded into my being.

This is the kind of experience worth recalling. Why? Because it reminds us that we have already accessed wisdom beyond logic. Jesus spoke about needing to become "like a little child." Remember moments from your own childhood and know that they live within you still.

new thinking

As I've mentioned, Albert Einstein said, "We can't solve our problems with the same thinking that we used to create them." I wonder what he would say today? My guess is that he would be shouting aloud while pointing to the life-threatening problems our old thinking has produced. He might also recite his definition of insanity: "doing the same thing over and over again and expecting a different result."

Here's a simple proposition: think differently to produce different behaviors and achieve different results. The conscious mind — our most daunting saboteur — has something to say about this: "What, me change?"

We've all sung that tune. It's arrogant: "This is what I believe and that's that!" It's disingenuous: "I could be wrong (fat chance!)." It's dismissive: "What value could come from that?"

What would new thinking actually *be* like and what real world difference might such thinking make? If we now take Einstein's radical proposal to heart, how will we begin?

escape the drama triangle

Many of us are well versed in the "drama triangle," complete with its three rotating roles: victim, persecutor, and rescuer. This frames old thinking in a context that often casts us as helpless victims dependent on a someone else to save us.

Salvation comes in many forms. You can take your pick from charismatic leaders to relationships to money, and success, but there is always a price tag for deliverance: our freedom. We become indebted to what saves us, pitted against what threatens us, and resigned to our role as a victim.

This describes the human dilemma, where we struggle to survive. Life was never meant to be like this. Life was meant to be enjoyable and rewarding and meaningful. And, that's exactly what life *can* become.

We can learn to think differently.

We can retire from being victims. We can even give up our rescuer role — fixing problems as clever, independent individuals competing with each other. Instead, we can access the genius of whole intelligence and thrive together.

Who programs us to be victims? Parents, teachers, politicians, entertainers, hate radio egomaniacs, not to mention all those voices inside our own heads. Notice how the word "they" lands as you read this. It's automatic to assign a persecutor role. That's the Drama Triangle in action. We judge, fear, and blame ... automatically.

"They" means bad guys. But I didn't suggest "they" were evil. They are as enslaved as the rest of us.

Challenge that knee jerk reaction into victimhood, which often begins with pointing a finger. Shun the other two substitute identities (perpetrator and rescuer) as well. This supports your shift into a new identity, connected within the whole of life.

Bowl or marble, remember? What's it going to be?

I am five, eating dinner with mother and two younger brothers.
"Mother," I ask, "where did I come from?" She's puzzled, annoyed.
"What? You were born in the Calgary General Hospital."

I'm doubtful. "No, I mean, where did I really come from, before that?"
Mother is perplexed. "Eat your mashed potatoes."

un-spelling

Let's identify four specific components of our old thinking.

> **Separation.** We are disconnected from the community of life by our belief in human exceptional-ism. We believe without question that humans are the most intelligent species ... we don't even need God (except to justify our behavior)! Narcissism rules.

> **Manipulation**. We are programmed into apathy, trained to fit in and behave, to become spectators in our own lives, which are shaped and controlled by others.

> **Amnesia**. We are persuaded to forget we are creators and become consumers instead. Meaning drains from our lives. "Everyone must believe in something; I believe I'll have another beer" is more than the slogan on a T-shirt, it's an amnesiac's mantra for the meaninglessness gobbling that fuels our dysfunctional economy.

> **Poverty**. We may grumble about wealth inequity but continue to support and invest in a system that depends on slave labor. The system seems to offer few viable options to impoverished hand-to-mouth struggle for an increasing majority.

These are not problems for the invisible puppet masters pulling our strings. Business-as-usual is not something that uncaring elected and corporate leaders wish to change. Why would we expect *any* change to start with them? Why would they tamper with what's worked for centuries to keep the elite empowered and the rest of us enslaved?

The long-term price of modern feudalism may be a home planet unfit for human habitation but they don't care. They are parasites getting while the getting's good, eventually killing off their host,.

Here's another opportunity to gut check for judgment. Are you blaming or observing as you read these words? Feeling outrage is normal; what we do with that energy makes the difference between a quantum activist and just another complainer.

Let's un-spell for a moment.

Instead of feeling anger towards "them," consider pity. The characters I described are slaves to power and comfort. They're whores, bought and paid for by people we've never heard of. They sit atop the food chain, sometimes carrying out their pillaging for profit under the guise of public service. They cannot be happy when they know they are just rich thieves.

What joy comes to them voluntarily?

You can pay for love but that isn't real love and there's no friendship involved. A thousand bucks can buy plenty but what happens when the money is gone? These shadow players don't intend to find out.

There *are* many powerful, wealthy individuals who do good in the world; I've met scores of them and they inspire me. But there are also legions of narcissistic, lying deniers consciously manipulating to maintain excessive lifestyles at any cost, to others and to the environment.

We can't fight them and win because it's their game. They know the rules and how to break them. They have the money and the power to keep us out of their club. We must think differently. For instance, rather than ignoring their influence or railing against them, we can realize, as Aleksandr Solzhenitsyn wrote, "The line dividing good and evil cuts through the heart of every human being." [3] That includes me ... and you.

forgiveness

One way to escape the drama triangle is to forgive.

Forgiveness is not something victims do. It's not always the domain of the rescuer either, because he or she is often demonizing someone else to justify their role and forgiveness is the last thing they would offer to a perpetrator of evil. However, forgiveness *is* the very thing that can un-spell us and collapse the drama triangle.

"What if?" Imagine, forgiving unconditionally. Is that even possible?

The Dali Lama forgives the Chinese, regardless of how they have hurt him and Tibet. Why? Because he is connected to universal intelligence. He is experiencing an adoring relationship with the Divine that overflows as an expression of unconditional love. The Dalai Lama is living what I call "The Transformational Lifestyle," which we will learn more about soon.

In the human world of disconnection and cruelty, His Holiness remains steadfastly connected and loving. I have friends who know him personally and they assure me he's the real deal. Well, we're in this human family with the Dalia Lama. We are fruit on the same tree, each of us ripening at our own, perfect time. Embrace this possibility for yourself.

His Holiness knows the secret a slave would never consider: real freedom requires liberating one's captors from the prison of our judgment. Scores of courageous prisoners have taught us this (Nelson Mandela, Aung San Suu Kyi, Mohammed Ali, etc.).

Let "them" be; we have bigger fish to fry, namely, learning how to think differently and focus our attention / intention to accelerate personal and global transformation. I devote all of Chapter Seven to thinking but you already know enough to begin thinking differently as you read.

wisdom

That chair you're sitting on, the screen or book you're reading, your very existence, *everything* began with imagination. After all, what got your mother and father together?

Imagination comes to focus through attention.

The modern spiritual author, Eckhart Tolle, wrote:

> Wisdom is not a product of thought. The deep *knowing* that is wisdom arises through the simple act of giving someone or something your full attention. Attention is primordial intelligence, consciousness itself. It dissolves the barriers created by conceptual thought, and with this comes the recognition that nothing exists in and by itself. It joins the perceiver and the perceived in a unifying field of awareness. It is the healer of separation. [4]

As Tolle said, "Nothing exists in and by itself." That includes you and me. This fact is systematically obliterated during the process of individuation every child is subjected to. We are taught, trained, brain washed, and indoctrinated into separation. We grow up and take our place in a world of fragmentation, where knowledge about how to succeed as a separate being is believed essential for achieving a satisfying life.

Back up and read Tolle's comment again. Better yet, I'll repeat it here, at least the part we can use as a springboard for this exploration of imagination: "...wisdom arises through the simple act of giving someone or something your full attention. Attention is primordial intelligence, consciousness itself. It dissolves the barriers created by conceptual thought..."

Conceptual thought generates separation; full attention accesses primordial intelligence. Not accidentally, life in the twenty-first century is all about deliberately fragmented attention. Stimulation tugs at us from every direction and the average human attention span has dropped to eight seconds, less than that of a gold fish! [5]

attention

The same article where I found that statistic also mentioned that "77% of people aged eighteen to twenty-four responded "yes" when asked, 'When nothing is occupying my attention, the first thing I do is reach for my phone.'"

What's experienced via a screen, any screen, is fundamentally different from the multi-dimensional environment we live in. The very idea that "nothing is occupying my attention" underlines separation. How could nothing be occupying my attention? Is nothing happening?

Is nothing happening until I focus my eyes on a screen?

Anyone who has experimented with mind-altering drugs knows how much *is* happening in any given moment. Substances that temporarily disable perception filters unleash an avalanche of sensory data, simply by expanding awareness. There's actually too much going on to pay attention to it all. So, what are we routinely filtering out? Nature, for one.

Wouldn't connection be something to educate our children in? Instead, we teach separation and we've become so skilled at it that separation has now become the norm. John Taylor Gatto — named New York City Teacher of the Year in 1989, 1990, and 1991, and New York State Teacher of the Year in 1991 [6] — wrote:

> Why, then, are we locking kids up in an involuntary network with strangers for twelve years? Surely not so a few of them can get rich? Even if it worked that way, and I doubt that it does, why wouldn't any sane community look on such education as positively wrong? It divides and classifies people, demanding that they compulsively compete with each other, and publicly labels losers by literally de-grading them, identifying them as "low-class" material. And the bottom line for the winners is that they can buy more stuff!
>
> I don't believe that anyone who thinks about that feels comfortable with such a silly conclusion. I can't help feeling that if we could only answer the question of what it is that we want from these kids we lock up, we would suddenly see where we took a wrong turn. I have enough faith in American imagination and resourcefulness to believe that at that point we'd come up with a better way – in fact, a whole supermarket of better ways. [7]

Imagine, as he conjectures, "a whole supermarket of better ways." If only we were open to the possibilities. It might help to say, "What if?"

restoring coherence

Apparently this is something we could learn from bacteria, according to Stephen Harrod Buhner in *Plant Intelligence and The Imaginal Realm*.

> Bacteria are, literally, remaking themselves in response to antibiotics. As soon as they encounter an antibiotic that can affect them, however minutely, they begin generating possible solutions to it. The variety and number of solutions they can generate are immense, from inactivating the part of the bacterial cell that the antibiotic is designed to destroy, to pumping the antibiotic out of their cells just as fast as it comes in, to altering the nature of their cellular wall to make them more impervious, to even using the antibiotic for food. [8]

What if we could adapt as fast as bacteria do?

Imagine being that nimble, individually and together. A threat appears? We react. A possibility emerges? We explore. Facts surface that contradict accepted wisdom? We research with open minds.

What if…. we could create a different world? It would take imagination willingness and courage. Plus, a different understanding of who "we" are.

In *The Field*, Lynne McTaggart writes:

> Our natural state of being is a relationship – a tango – a constant state of one influencing the other. Just as the subatomic particles that compose us cannot be separated from the space and particles surround them, so living beings cannot be separated from each other. A living system of greater coherence could exchange information and create or restore coherence in a disordered, random, or chaotic system. [9]

I am speeding towards the US Canada border crossing, having just picked up the mail from our post office box. Suddenly, inexplicably, I begin weeping, tears of joy.

I learn later that in those exact same moments, several of my colleagues were discussing the idea of an educational program for teenagers and deciding that I should help develop it.

Doing exactly that became one of the most emotionally rewarding learning adventures of my life.

the 80 / 20 rule

Many of us are familiar with the 80/20 Rule, or The Pareto principle, which was developed by management consultant Joseph M. Juran. The principle, which Juran named after a nineteenth century Italian economist, states that about 80% of effects arise from 20% of the causes.

Pareto observed this rule applying to many situations. For instance, he noted that 80% of the land in Italy in his time was owned by 20% of the population. He also noticed that 20% of the pea pods in his garden contained 80% of the peas. It's become an accepted understanding in business that 80% of sales tend to come from 20% of the clients. [10]

It's probably a conservative estimate that 80% of our thinking is negative while 20% is positive. And how about the media? What is the positive /

negative ratios there? And how do we balance our thinking? By expanding our minds. The simplest way to do that is to ask "What if?" I also recommend that you experiment with the following imaginal workout, courtesy of the Queen from *Alice in Wonderland*.

> Alice said: "One can't believe impossible things."
>
> "I daresay you haven't had much practice," said the Queen. "When I was your age, I always did it for half-an-hour a day. Why, sometimes I've believed as many as six impossible things before breakfast." [11]

You can exercise your imaginal muscles by creating a few imaginative narratives each day. Here's an example:

I sprout a dorsal fin, dive into Lithia Creek, and swim upstream as far as I can, then rocket from the water with immense wings and climb to a great height.

I turn into a giant stone and plummet into the stream, creating a deep crater and exploding thousands of diamonds in the fiery impact. They fall back down into the hands of hikers on the trail who become instant millionaires.

You could begin with something much simpler, like:

I start my car, which immediately turns into a horse. We gallop across a foggy marsh towards a far off castle. The castle becomes a giant marshmallow and I disappear inside.

Start simple and go wilder every time. Enjoy manufacturing craziness to flush your imagination from its comfort zone. Feel yourself hitting that "blank mind" wall and then flying right through it. You must be made of a different material to do that. So, what are you made of?

As Pablo Picasso said, "Everything you can imagine is real." So, use your imagination.

What if?

೬

*If you believe that you are NOT omnipresent, omniscient
and ultimately omnipotent – you are delusional.*

*If you believe that you are separate from that which you call God,
then you are living a lie.*

~ Kevin Michel

3

intention

*... human thoughts and intentions
are an actual physical 'something'
with the astonishing power to change our world.
Every thought we have is a tangible energy
with the power to transform.
A thought is not only a thing;
a thought is a thing that influences other things.*

~ Lynne McTaggart

Biologist Lyall Watson wrote *Lifetide* in 1980, presenting the work of Japanese primatologists who had been studying Macaque monkeys. They noticed an odd behavior, which Ken Keyes brought into the mainstream the next year with his book, *The Hundredth Monkey Effect.*

Here's the short story: a few monkeys started washing potatoes before they ate them. The new habit spread slowly. But when the hundredth monkey (an arbitrary figure, the researchers didn't count) joined in, suddenly monkeys on neighboring islands started doing it too. [1]

Keyes wrote, "... this Hundredth Monkey Phenomenon means that when only a limited number of people know of a new way, it may remain the conscious property of these people. But there is a point at which if only one more person tunes in to a new awareness, a field is strengthened so that this awareness is picked up by almost everyone!" [2] Watson clarified that not all the nearby monkeys adopted the new habit, just some of them did.

Well, something affected you and me and we owe big thanks to those who've been "washing their potatoes" for many years before us. These earth warriors are the real inspiration, people like Joanna Macy, Wangari

Maathai, Richard Attenborough, Erin Brockovich, Julia Butterfly Hill, James Lovelock, Lester R. Brown, etc.

We also find plenty of inspiration from our non-human colleagues: As the International Whaling Commission met to debate the future of whaling, marine biologists said that whales are similar to humans in their capacity to feel and suffer.

> *Recent studies show that whales—like great apes and dolphins— possess a self-awareness, which one neurobiologist says allows them to experience emotional suffering as well as physical pain.In one experiment, a neurobiologist placed a small mark on dolphins' bodies and had them look at themselves in the mirror. The dolphins reacted to the image and looked at the spot on their bodies, showing they have a sense of self-identity, she said. Brain activity shows they also engage in a form of social interaction some scientists call culture: "Evidence is growing that for at least some cetacean species, culture is both sophisticated and important," a Canadian professor told the Daily Telegraph.* [3]

our turn

Quantum activists impact the "field" we share with all species through energetic transmission. I've been referring to The Wonder Field, where qualities can be broadcast to stimulate transformation. This skill is centered by our favorite question: "What if...?"

Quantum activists in training – and there are millions of us, we just haven't identified with the term – are already collaborating unconsciously with every other new thinking innovator. The transformation we are undergoing personally is a real time species-wide event. Every choice and every action, every thought and feeling, everything that arises from the burning passion of our commitment to contribute, impacts this field we share. The Wonder Field resonates with our imaginative attention and intentions.

I'm big on measurable goals. So, I propose that we target a specific date – May 1, 2025 – and focus our quantum activist efforts towards a New World Party on that day. No worries, there will still be lots to do after that but this gives us a near-term goal to reach for.

Here's my radical proposal: Could a sufficient amount of focused intention streaming through imaginative social enterprises contribute to a transformational moment in consciousness for humanity?

It is May 1, 2025.

I am 75 years old, spry and alert, deeply excited as news pours in of the many thousands of colleagues tuning in for our New World Party.

We've outgrown our dependency on digital technologies to connect us. In silent communion, we consciously engage together in The Wonder Field, our familiar meeting place.

One by one, quantum activists report in. Evidence of verified success with social, political, and spiritual change is presented and the feeling grows: Something wonderful is happening!

science weighs in

Biologist Rupert Sheldrake exposed ten false assumptions of science in his book, *Setting Science Free*. Larry Dossey, M.D., author of *Reinventing Medicine* wrote of Sheldrake: "Rupert Sheldrake may be to the twenty-first century what Charles Darwin was to the nineteenth: someone who sent science spinning in wonderfully new and fertile directions." [4]

Blogger Mike Adams unbundles Sheldrake's perspective:

> There appears to be a 'driving creative force' behind much of what we observe in nature, including in animals and humans. This driving creative force, if you get right down to it, appears to have a connection with spirit — a non-physical 'mind' which gives consciousness to physical beings of all kinds.

> What we see in the natural world — in ecosystems, plants, animals and even humans — is not explainable through natural selection alone. There exists intention, consciousness, and a seeming desire to achieve complex goals by taking fantastic evolutionary leaps that modern science cannot explain. As a simple example of this, consider the fact that although many thousands of humanoid-like fossils have been unearthed in the last two centuries, there are still no fossils that record the

theoretical 'missing link' which is supposed to link humans to primates. Why have no such fossils been found? Almost certainly because they do not exist. [5]

what's possible and when ?

If a new human past emerges – proving that we did not evolve gradually from apes – another possibility appears for the future. If we suddenly became what we are now at some point in the past, could we not also become something radically different at some point in the future, and just as suddenly?

What are humans destined to become and when? Is there a viable option beyond becoming just another extinct species? Most intriguingly, could this transformation be experienced simultaneously by strangers thousands of miles from each other?

The Hungarian mathematician Farkas Bolyai advised his son, "When the time is ripe for certain things, they appear at different places in the manner of violets coming to light in early spring." This suggests simultaneous manifestations in form that are natural, uncontrived, and spontaneous.

Back to the monkey story. Imagine if a monkey had grumbled, "What can one monkey do?" Of course, he wasn't consciously washing his potato in order to transmit the habit to others. If the potato tasted better and he had a conscience, he might have wished others could enjoy the same experience, but that's not why he did it.

He wanted to do it. He desired a better tasting potato.

Similarly, the vast majority of change makers on the planet are "doing the right thing" because they want to. Everyone's contributions add up. Is there a tipping point to come? Change and transformation could come in an instant, defying logic and belief, proven real the moment it happens. Something could happen on May 1, 2025. Or not. But what a grand adventure to imagine something magnificent like that...

What if?

Start thinking now about who you want to invite to the party.

failure is not so bad

Years ago I was conducting a seminar on stress management in New York and said, "Imagine you've just been given a terminal diagnosis. The doctor tells you that you have twelve months to live, maximum. You attend a seminar like this or read a book and get inspired. You decide to try out what the 'expert' is advocating. You discover research that suggests becoming happy can improve health. So, you watch funny movies, listen to comedians, and laugh for hours every day. Twelve months go by and you die on the very day your doctor advised that you would."

I remember staring out at the puzzled faces and delivering the punchline: "Wouldn't you be angry that you wasted a whole year being happy when you could have been miserable?"

They laughed. They got it.

The experiment I am proposing may or may not get the physical results we hope for: catalyzing a transformative shift of some kind for humanity. After all, that's a wildly grandiose ambition. But why not enjoy the journey?

inventing reality

You're learning how to focus intention to develop imaginative scenarios in your life, merging emotion and logic to heal your past, create your future and enjoy the present.

Imagined success can become more real than imagined failure. Why not? After all, the question, "What if?" can be applied as easily to positives as to negatives.

"What if we don't have enough money for rent this month?" OK, how about: "What if we have more than enough money for rent this month?" I hear the cynical protests. "Day dreaming is a waste of time." Of course, I agree that *just* daydreaming or speaking words changes nothing. But where might they lead?

A blogger pointed out: "Daydreaming and downtime can lead to solutions for difficult scientific problems and provide inspiration for creative works. Some of history's best-known scientific and literary achievements grew out of such mental meandering." 6

I found a site that lists famous inventions that originated in dreams. Elias Howe invented the sewing machine in 1845. He got the idea in a horrendous murder dream. A teenaged Albert Einstein dreamed of electrocuted cows. Years later he came up with his signature general theory of relativity and referenced that dream as the source. Film director James Cameron was a nobody in 1981 when he had a "fever dream" and concocted the whole idea for the Terminator movies. 7

Real results depend on a million factors and many other people, all of which are beyond our control. What's *always* available is our imagination. We can dream and we can learn how to turn those dreams into reality by using focused intention. This idea isn't new but my particular formula is.

show me the intention

Spud Webb won the 1986 NBA slam-dunk competition. He was just 5' 7" yet he beat fellow Atlanta Hawk team mate Dominique Wilkins, the defending champion, who stood 6' 8." Webb overcame 11" height disadvantage and won with a vertical leap of 42 inches. He was described as having 'springs in his legs.' 8

Webb was born into poverty in Texas. He was short. He was black. He made it to the NBA, became a star, and won that competition. 3 How did he do that? I'll guarantee you that he had a vision and he had an intention. He asked, "What if?" He conceptualized a highly unlikely possibility and then worked hard to achieve it.

Imagine this conversation. "So Spud, you're sixteen now, what are you planning to do with your life?"

"I'm going to play basketball in the NBA."

Or, he could have said: "Well, I really love playing basketball but I'm short so that's not going to happen. Let's see, I'm poor and I'm not a genius so, I dunno, I guess I'll start to look for a job. Any ideas?" He could have complained, accepting his shortcomings as insurmountable obstacles.

I wonder how many Spud Webb's are out there in your circle, how much greatness is suffocating under negative beliefs that kill imaginative genius before it can empower intention? Maybe you could do something about that.

"What if..?" is a great conversation starter. It can open the door to creating an intention. First, you counter residual negativity – in yourself and others – by posing an imaginative, positive possibility. Then you focus your dream into a specific intention. Doing that for ourselves may encourage others to do the same.

if you can imagine it ...

Where did Spud Webb get his insights and confidence?

We can credit an angel, his intuition, or maybe he had an encouraging grandfather or early school coach who mentored his development. But he also had his body, an amazing resource that all of us have but rarely consult.

In his wonderful book, *What is Your Body Telling You?* Steve Sisgold writes: "By disconnecting from our brilliant bodies and abandoning ourselves, we lose our natural confidence. We grow more reluctant to take risks. We lose the ability to feel and acknowledge our deepest feelings and the courage to speak our truth. And we continue to deny and repress our feelings to protect ourselves.

"Pain, shame, fear, sadness, confusion, and aloneness are the result. Fear, denial, and disconnection from our body and our feelings become an unconscious, self-protective habit, a default response to life. The innermost self is abandoned. Instead of playing full out, many of us begin to play it safe, or play not to lose." [9]

You're probably not going to play basketball in the NBA, but you *can* play full out on the field where you live. If you're treading water, you're not fully alive, you're just existing.

Engagement is always just a choice away.

---

another mind blower from nature

There are phenomena known as atmospheric rivers, that is, narrow bands of water vapor a mile above the ocean, that extend for thousands of miles. Theuy exist, much like rivers on the land or rivers that flow through the oceans, carrying water and life over long distances. Occasionally, they begin to pour onto the land beneath them. In 1862 they poured onto California causing rains that lasted for forty-three days. The Central Valley turned into an inland sea three-hundred miles long and twenty miles wide. [10]

Take a moment to reread those words. "Atmospheric rivers... that extend for thousands of miles." What an image! It's difficult to visualize that — And that vast inland sea? 1861 is not that long ago. Again, it is hard to imagine.

Why do I include this reference? Because it's a mind blower and we need our minds blown — regularly. Why? So we can free ourselves from conventional thinking and ask What If?

Asking "What if?" could be a key to our personal and species survival because conventional thinking has exhausted so many tried-and-untrue approaches. Surely it's time to attempt something radically different.

debating the future

Since Al Gore's 1996 documentary film, *An Inconvenient Truth*, won an Oscar, some of his predictions have materialized while others have not. Climate change deniers, often financed by billionaires heavily invested in the fossil fuel industry (and committed to maintaining the status quo at all costs) have converted facts into uncertainty.

Climate change has become a public debate, regardless of actual temperature rise, ice melts, killer storms, etc., even though, as one blogger wrote, "Only 16% of Americans believe there is not enough evidence to prove global climate change is real, the lowest percentage since a survey began asking the question in 2008." [11]

Mainstream media, controlled by corporations invested in old thinking and committed to delaying change, tell a different story, manufacturing doubt where there is none by falsely stating that scientists *aren't* in agreement, when they almost universally are. Spin propaganda succeeds in slowing change, even as smart entrepreneurs rave about the potential gold rush of renewable energy business.

We are not rational creatures. We are rationalizing creatures.

Here's the thing: We do not change because of facts; it's emotion that sways us. Trying to motivate "green" behavior by telling people how bad things are and how much worse they could get simply doesn't motivate, at least, not for long. What *does* motivate is a compelling vision of desirable future possibilities. But it must be so appealing that we come to want it more than we want the alluring distraction of the moment.

We stay motivated longer and invest more passion when we are *for* something then when we are *against* something.

Quoting further from the same online article, "The truth may be inconvenient, but it's our truth, one that we all share in a finite planet. If there is one lesson from history we may apply here, is that denial is never an efficient long-term strategy." [12]

What if?

What if you could face challenges with imagination and construct clear intentions for the future you want? I wonder what magic might occur?

ॐ

What if you slept?
And what if in your sleep, you dreamed?

And what if you dreamed you went to heaven
and there plucked a strange and beautiful flower?

And what if, when you woke, you held the flower in your hand?

Ha! What then?

~ Samuel Taylor Coleridge

4

imagifi

The important thing is to not stop questioning.
Curiosity has its own reason for existence.
One cannot help but be in awe when he contemplates
the mysteries of eternity, of life,
of the marvelous structure of reality.
It is enough if one tries merely to comprehend
a little of this mystery each day.

~ Albert Einstein

I invented the term "imagifi" years ago, without fully knowing what it meant and long before I decided to invent words and seed a language for new thinking. Now the meaning has become obvious: use imagination to "imagifi" any situation by making something novel of it.

As a comedian said, "I started out as a child." We all did, and that meant imagifying everything automatically. Before we could think or speak, we wondered, "What would it be like if I put this in my mouth?" What would it be like to climb up there, what would it be like to touch that, what would it be like to scream, to laugh, etc?" We went for experience after experience and they were all novel. That's how we learned.

At first.

Then we went to school. Even before that, a thousand influences began to transform us from creators (of our own experience) to consumers (buying someone else's). "Individuation" is the process that results in us becoming a distinct individual. It turns out that there's a fundamental flaw in *how* we individuate.

French philosopher Gilbert Simonton wrote about "pre-individual fields," which "make individuation possible. Individuation is an ever-incomplete process, always leaving a 'pre-individual' left over, which makes possible future individuations." [1] Simonton was talking about atoms but we can apply the same principle to humans, since we are made of atoms. If future individuations remain possible, then we are never done.

Becoming an adult is not the end of growing up. What is this "pre-individual," this persistent essence of ourselves that is ever ready to individuate in new ways? It suggests an essence that doesn't change, plus a process of eternal evolution, rebirth, becoming ever different than we were before while remaining the same at our core.

How many adults do you know who feel that way about themselves? Do you?

How could life ever be boring if this was our experience? Who needs tons of stuff when ongoing personal transformation is available? What if we possesses an innate genius potential, proven by our ability to continue individuating?

Lynne McTaggart writes in *The Field*: "What we call 'genius' may simply simply be a greater ability to access the Zero Point Field. In that sense, our intelligence, creativity, and imagination are not locked in our brains but exist as an interaction within The Field." [2] This author describes what she is referring to as the Zero Point Field or just The Field. I call it The Wonder Field.

living in wonder

In The Wonder Field, questions are more important than answers and discovery is the goal of our every day adventures. When you ask "what if?" you embark on a learning adventure. How much education do we get about this? Not so much. Instead, we rush towards answers and get rewarded for memorizing the old, not discovering the new.

> *My wife and I are walking through the woods that surround our home. Spontaneously and for no obvious reason she says, "Let's find a four leaf clover."*
>
> *The moment I hear those words I stop, bend, and point. My finger aims squarely at ... a four-leaf clover! There is no searching, no engaging the usual thinking process. She asks, "What if?" and nature answers.*

I recall the feeling of that experience. It was effortless. We tapped into some kind of magic. Where did her idea to find a four leaf clover come from? I can't remember her ever suggesting we look for one before. But on that day, at that exact place on the trail, she did. And ... there it was. That's what can happen when we live in wonder.

Intention brings what we access through wonder into focus. That's the imagifying process. I invented a more precise term for describing how this works: "focus proximity."

focus proximity

Imagine you are outside on a sunny day. You lay a piece of paper on the ground and hover over it with a magnifying glass. First, you lay the glass directly on top of the paper and nothing happens. Next, you hold the lens three feet above the paper. Again, nothing happens. Now you jockey the lens into position, adjusting to locate the exact distance where the magnifying glass can focus the sun's rays on the paper. You find that point and start a fire.

This is focus proximity. It's how quantum activists focus power.

We find the appropriate "distance" from whatever we put our attention on. We focus our intention – experimenting to find the correct "distance" — and spark change.

In pain, under pressure, our learned habit is to deny, avoid, or overdo. We pull back or we over-indulge. We ignore the problem and hope it will go away on its own. Or, if two pills are good, we assume that taking four would be better, right?

But what would the correct "distance" be?

In my magnifying glass example, having the raw materials wasn't enough. Sun, lens, and paper were all there but nothing happened until s the correct focus was determined. Similarly, we *have* everything that we need to catalyze change, even transformation. We simply need to learn how to focus our attention/intention and "imagifi.'"

Learning how to imagifi is meant to become a habit we learn, master, and use every day. This is what turns our personal Wonder Field from an empty warehouse into a fun farm bursting with imaginal life forms. But where do we find the raw material to populate our Wonder Field?

As Thomas Berry poetically instructs:

> The inner life of the human depends immediately on the other world. Only if the human imagination is activated by the flight of the great soaring birds in the heavens, by the blossoming flowers of earth, by the awesome sight of the sea, by the lightning and thunder of the great storms that breakthrough the heat of summer; only then will the deep inner experiences be evoked within the human soul."[3]

I am returning home from town and begin pulling off the road to check the mailbox just outside our driveway. But a car is in my way, stopped in the middle of the road. My momentary irritation melts as the driver motions excitedly. I follow his gesture, staring into the woods. "There," he exclaims, "right there, on that branch!"

It takes me awhile to see it, the largest owl I've ever found in these woods. He is twelve feet away, staring at us, unblinking, majestic. We sit, enthralled. Cars pass, slowing in curiosity. The owl doesn't budge.

This stranger and I share a few words. After a few minutes, he drives away. Immediately, the owl takes flight, expertly maneuvering his immense wingspan through the trees.

I reflect. How did that driver see the owl as he drove by? I could barely see it when I knew something was there, when he pointed it out, and I had stopped my car. And why did the owl leave when he did? Passing traffic hadn't moved him.

Perhaps these two beings were connected and had just honored a date they made to meet in the woods that day. Or, this could just be another entertaining example of randomness alive in the universe.

missing the signs

Intention can be focused to create a single hoped-for result or it can provide a context for a series of initiatives. PART TWO is about turning on, getting activated, and exploring the various kinds of intentions we can employ. But I wanted to tell a short story here about what can happen when an overriding intention is not in place or when it's ignored.

It's easy to miss important signs. In this case, that's exactly what I did.

I wake up, get out of bed, and fall over. The world spins around me violently and my stomach churns with nausea. Am I having a stroke, a heart attack, what's happening to me?

My wife drives me to the hospital. All the rooms are full so I lay on a cot in the hallway. An MRI confirms it's not a stroke. A doctor asks me questions and suggests this could be positional vertigo. He gives me the obligatory drugs and assures me that I will recover fully.

Let's hit the pause button. Just prior to the drugging, my wife said, "Let's get out of here." I'd be proud to tell you that I listened but I didn't. I was still caught up in fear. So, I took the drugs as prescribed. After an hour or so of little to no improvement we left. My wife intuited that we should call a friend for help. Our friend suggested that we visit our food coop to pick up a specific homeopathic remedy.

I am sitting in the passenger seat as we drive home, my eyes squeezed shut, feeling those tiny pills dissolve under my tongue. Thirty seconds later I am feeling immense relief. This is the medicine I needed.

What if I had known what my wife did when she knew it? Her "what if?" muscle was stronger than mine that day. So, I learned. Whether that one lesson was worth the $3,400 hospital bill is debatable.

It takes something to reflect back on a missed beat, to study the moments where myopia or delusion hid an important "fact," and to create the conscious intention to do different/better next time.

two choices

Two choices emerge relative to the application of intention in The Wonder Field:

1. Ignore "what if" possibilities and continue as a disempowered individual, using old thinking to wrestle with problems and remain woefully unable to contribute towards innovative, positive change in your personal life or further afield.

2. Discover, learn, and master how to focus intention and become expert at imagifying your real life situations; living a transformational lifestyle.

Had I been stronger and clearer with my intention that day, I would have divined, as my wife did, that what was happening in the hospital was not in resonance with my own personally authored "reality."

That's a heavy word, I know. In fact, I remember a friend once joking that "reality is for people who can't handle drugs." I use the word to describe what's happening now, which I believe to be highly fluid and amenable to our conscious adjustments.

divine magic

The concept of conscious intention working magic is not new. Whether it's rubbing a lamp to gain three wishes, praying in church, repeating positive affirmations, applying the so-called Law of Attraction, or using some formula from the scores of self-help books such as seven habits, six laws, four keys, etc., most of us accept the notion that consciously focusing intention can create results.

I've introduced the fact that every result we achieve begins invisibly with imagination and intention. There's a third factor which really comes first.

> *In his book about sacred activism, The Hope, Andrew Harvey quotes one of his mentors, Bede Griffiths, who writes: "There are a few beings on earth, I believe, who have reached such a humble level of union with God that what they will in prayer is granted, because what they will and what the Divine wills is the same."* 4

First, Griffiths alerts us to a remarkable achievement that some rare individuals have apparently made. "What they will in prayer is granted." But, before we demand the formula, listen to what he adds: "What they will and what the Divine wills is the same." For this formula to work, then, individual thinking must be aligned with Divine thinking.

That's done with prayer and will. This is the inner code for a quantum activist.

Feeling awed is different than feeling intimidated, as one might feel upon entering a grand church. Back to our marble and bowl... which are you? Being enraptured with our connection to Spirit is a natural experience.

In our consumer culture we have traded that direct connection for middleman leaders (priests, gurus, political leaders) and stuff. The unmediated connection to Spirit is what Griffiths is speaking of. It can't be borrowed, bought, or sold but his use of the word "will" certainly implies being proactive. So, he's telling us that when these special individuals pray in some particular way and then act, the Divine acts through them, producing results.

Might this be possible for us? Could what *we* will "in prayer" through our focused intention produce Divine results? Doesn't this possibility redefine humans as agents for the Divine, not victims struggling to fix problems in a dangerous world? Finally, could this coherent creativity be accomplished by more than a handful of sainted extraordinaire's?

Let's study his full formula.

Note again the concluding part of Griffiths's comment: "... what they will and what the Divine wills is the same." This is a far cry from: "I want what I want so I 'will' it into existence. It's for my benefit, perhaps for my family, my community, even the entire world."

The "good" benefits of the intention (for oneself) is the problem. The road to Hell is paved with good intentions and it doesn't matter if those heading in that direction validate their self-willed actions by namedropping God.

the myopia of personal success

"God wants you to be rich," raves the evangelist to his eager congregation. Why on earth would God want you to be rich? Imagine if we were *all* rich. The planet can't sustainably supply our material desires as it is; being even more successful consumers would produce an apocalyptical nightmare. Oh, wait, it already has.

Here is what often remains unasked in the domain of intention setting: "What about Divine will?" Who is able to align a personal intention with Divine intention? This is fundamentally different than selfish desire or even selfless service. God may not actually want you to have a 7,000 sq. ft. mansion. Sorry.

The book, *Think and Grow Rich*, authored by Napoleon Hill in 1937, has sold over seventy million copies. It's become the Bible for super achievers, a sure-fire blueprint for individual success. Hill writes, "You are the master of your destiny. You can influence, direct, and control your own environment. You can make your life what you want it to be." [5]

And that's exactly what we try to do, following a host of successful self improvement experts intent on accelerating our speed towards a cliff called near-term human extinction. But I doubt many of these experts would admit their error. Old thinking has worked fine for them, it's generated wealth and fame. How could encouraging others to follow in their footsteps be wrong? Only if they knew that there's a cliff ahead.

We strive for "success" by controlling our environment. Hill makes it clear how we can do that: "Life's battles don't always go to the stronger or faster man but sooner or later the man who wins is the man WHO THINKS HE CAN." Here's a perfect description of old thinking.

No. We are meant to act in harmony with the Divine, to surrender disconnected, ego-based fix-the-problem thinking, often fortified by religious concepts that champion human entitlement and "dominion." Can you entertain the possibility of becoming able to "act in harmony with the Divine," in every moment of your normal daily life? Is it intimidating to contemplate possessing such God-like qualities?

the unholy trinity

Yes, it's a leap to embrace such a personal possibility (and responsibility). I can hear the silent doubts. "Who, me?"

You've had the same disempowering "education" that I've had. But don't write yourself off. And, beware what I call The Unholy Trinity:

> 1. **God** *is a separate being, superior to humans.*
>
> 2. **Exceptional-ism**: *Humans are separate from nature, superior to all other species, created by a separate God to have dominion over all of them.*
>
> 3. **Individuality**: *Individual survival and success is a struggle and ultimately, we are on our own.*

People can get themselves killed for claiming oneness with God.

Jesus is way more popular on a cross than he ever was urging others to accept that when he said "the Father and I are one" he was talking about us too. There is nothing profane about developing our own personal connection with the Divine, without a middleman (including Jesus). In fact, it's arrogant to claim personal stature separate from the Divine.

Who are you, who am I, to disconnect from the power that beats our hearts? Who are we to attempt life on our own? Worshiping a theoretical, separate, superior God, even through His "representative" — whether that be Jesus or some guru — doesn't remedy our alienated destructiveness.

Just look where that old thinking has led us. Our assumed superiority over all other species is proving catastrophic. We continue to trumpet our magnificence while knowing next to nothing about what other species can do. To challenge this arrogance, I'll keep including factoids about species intelligence throughout these pages. Here's a beauty:

> The Clark's Nutcracker (bird) possesses a sublingual pouch in its throat in which it can store up to one hundred white pine seeds at a time ... When the pouch is full, the bird begins depositing the seeds in caches spread over an area of up to ten square miles... Some 30,000 seeds in 10,000 locations – two to five seeds each – are stored every year.... Researchers have found that the birds can remember the location of every seed cache for up to two years. [6]

If we're so much smarter than this bird, why can't we even remember where we put our car keys in a 1,500 square foot house an hour ago?

We can argue that humans build skyscrapers and jet airplanes. Animals can't do that. But animals aren't rendering the planet unfit for their own survival. That's the difference between how they create and how we create. What we call success doesn't factor in environmental impact. Yes, Round Up may be a successful pesticide (temporarily), but it's toxic for us too.

God, exceptional-ism, and individuality: let's challenge this unholy trinity of sacred cows so we can graduate to conscious creator status, focusing intention for holistically beneficial results as quantum activists.

a new mantra

Humanity may very well be accelerating towards a cliff of near-term extinction and individual success disconnected from "Divine will" can do no better than guarantee a long fall.

Let's blame French mathematician Rene Descartes, revered as the father of modern philosophy, who proclaimed: "I think, therefore I am." He elevated thinking disconnected from the Divine into a substitute position of supremacy.

Not such a good idea, after all, it turns out, some 400 years later.

Consider the results. If you need convincing, read this article from *The Nation*. It presents a clear-sighted analysis of where we stand today in terms of environmental threats to our survival. Here are two of their conclusions, one hopeful and one troubling:

1. The United States and China both appear to have reached a peak in energy-related emissions in recent years, largely by scaling back coal in favor of renewable energy.

2. Global emissions may have peaked—but temperatures are rising at record speed, threatening a massive sea-level rise that could destroy major cities by 2100. New studies have warned that sea levels could rise six to nine feet by 2100, or even sooner, according to retired NASA climate scientist James Hansen. This would inundate hundreds of coastal communities throughout the world, including New York City, Miami, and Washington, DC, as well as London, Hamburg, Lagos, Tokyo, Hong Kong, and Shanghai. [7]

For humanity to map a path to extended survival on a still hospitable planet, we need a conceptual transformation that aligns our thinking with the system that has worked successfully for millions of years: nature. We also need a new identity mantra. Instead of "I think, therefore I am," how about, "I think new, therefore I am new."

New thinking leads to new acting leads to new results, all arising from a new identity. Remember, who you are matters more than what you do.

Surely the urgency and severity of conditions on Spaceship Earth demand that we learn how to focus intention, to imagifi our challenges, to align our will with Divine will by trading dogmatic certainty for child-like curiosity, to think the way other species already do, and to become agents for the expression of the genius that abounds throughout creation.

> *Religions speak about the Kingdom of Heaven as a promised reward in the future, after we die. But that term also describes what is supposed to appear right here (on earth as it is in heaven), to experience right now.*

In the two years since the first edition of this book hit the streets, I've worked with hundreds of clients and delivered the program, in one form or another, to many small groups. Here's the primary lesson I've learned:

repetition is the key to success

Having a daily practice is essential. But who has time for that? You do, I do, we all do ... when we do it the right way. As you learn these seven practices and study the background material in each chapter – distributed with the intention of disrupting our addiction to linear input – you are creating new habits and growing quantum competency.

These seven practices will weave together inside you, to become one single practice which, once mastered, will provide for you what electricity does for your computer. You will use the practice to "start up" in the morning, to "re-start" whenever you encounter a problem during the day, and to "shut down" before you slip into the dream time.

Imagifi your life.

ॐ

I am touching the Kingdom of God with every step. When I touch the present moment deeply, I touch the Pure Land; I touch the ultimate, and I touch eternity. In deep contact with the Earth and wonders of life, I touch my true nature. The exquisite orchid flower, the ray of sunshine, and even my own miraculous body – if they do not belong to the Kingdom of God, what does?

Contemplating the Earth deeply, whether a floating cloud or a falling leaf, I can see the no-birth, no-death nature of reality. With you, dear Mother, we are carried into eternity. We have never been born and we will never die.

Once we have realized this, we can then appreciate and enjoy life fully, no longer afraid of aging or death, nor caught in complexes about ourselves, not yearning for things to be different than they are. We already are, and we already have, what we are looking for."

~ Thich Nhat Hanh

connection

I am made to love the pond and meadow,
as the wind is made to ripple the water.

~ Henry David Thoreau

We've just considered how to harness our imagination to imagifi our lives by focusing intention in a way that aligns us with Divine will. We ended the last chapter with a salute to nature from Thich Nhat Hanh.

Indeed, it's time to consult the expert. Let's do now what human beings have neglected to do for untold centuries: Let's ask our mother, Mother Nature.

Nature doesn't operate according to linear time like we do. Linear time, clock time, travels in a straight path from A to B to C. Past, present, and future proceed in a straight, measured line. By contrast, nature has seasons that cycle in what I call "deep time."

deep time

Deep time is a term that originated in the eighteenth century within scientific circles and has come to be associated with extremely long periods of pre-human history.

For instance, scientists estimate the earth is about 4.55 billion years old. Creationists counter that the Bible establishes Earth's age at 6,000 years, based on math that computes a biblical day of creation as, literally, twenty-four hours. Take your pick, beliefs or beliefs.

When you spend time in nature – an interesting way to put it – you soon abandon the world of beliefs; your mind slows into the rhythm of deep time in the natural world. Just being alive begins to feel different.

This is what we are exploring throughout PART ONE, the shift from linear time to deep time and how that feels. As you are noticing, this is not a linear process. We're meandering, which is nature's way.

consequences

Let's amble back to Thoreau's invitation. "...I am made to love..."

Love what?

The pond and the meadow — nature. This presents a polar opposite to the biblical attitude towards nature: "Let us make man in Our Image, according to Our likeness; and have dominion over the fish of the sea, and over the fowl of the air, and over the cattle, and over all the earth, and over every creeping thing that creepeth upon the earth." [1]

Dominion. Control. There's not much love in that holy injunction. As Napoleon Hill further declared, "You are the master of your destiny. You can influence, direct and control your own environment. You can make your life what you want it to be." [2]

We have succeeded. We have created a civilization that represents the aggregate of 7 billion individuals desires, fulfilled or frustrated. We stand atop the food chain, masters of creation, using our exceptionalist thinking to direct and control our environment.

Look at what this has *done* to the environment.

We have marauded like an invasive species with super powers. We have established ourselves as the most dangerous species by far in our not-so-blissful ignorance, and we are living with the global consequences.

aren't we special ?

"We once viewed ourselves as the only creatures with emotions, morality, and culture. But the more we investigate the animal kingdom, the more we discover that is simply not true. Many scientists are now convinced that all these traits, once considered the hallmarks of humanity, are also found in animals." [3]

Legend has it that Chief Seattle cautioned the white man to take care of animals. He said, "What is man without the beasts? If all the beasts were gone, men would die from great loneliness of spirit, for whatever happens to the beasts also happens to man. All things are connected. Whatever befalls the earth befalls the children of the earth." [4]

Historical records peg extinction rates over the past 300-400 years at about one species per year, 280 birds and mammals. Here in the twenty-first century, human activities have accelerated that rate astronomically, up to an estimated 10,000 species per year, now and into the future. [5]

The incredible but true fact is that nature, for many, is no more than an incidental backdrop. It's hard to ignore nature but we do, navigating hypnotically from bed to kitchen to car to office to restaurant to car to home, with a screen in front of us most of the time. Many of us do that almost every day. What might happen if we did more than take pictures of nature, hike through nature, and mourn nature's loss?

Here's one poet's answer: "When the natural world reawakens in every fiber of our being the primal knowledge of connection, and graces us with a few moments of sheer awe, it can shatter the hubris and isolation so necessary to narcissistic defenses." [6]

In the twenty-first century, the human species huddles in a narcissistic bubble that's running out of air. The urgent imperative is to burst through that bubble and connect, with nature and with the Divine. This is the most essential component of new thinking for quantum activists. We thrive on the sheer awe that permeates those domains. Both have the medicine to slow and perhaps halt our descent into the final act of this seemingly inevitable human tragedy.

Here's another nature factoid to continue chipping away at our human hubris: "... chimpanzees can sign up to 3,000 words (and even invent their own words for objects they haven't been taught words for) and then teach the ability to use sign language to their offspring..." [7]

success

I read *Success* magazine every month, to stay in touch with today's innovators. Frustrated as usual with their trademark neglect of nature, I finally wrote a letter to the editor, mentioning that I could probably scan the entire issue and not find the word "environment" more than a handful of times, and then most likely commenting on home offices.

"What about nature?" I complained, and got a nice email back. The editor agreed and published my letter. And, not surprisingly, twelve issues later, nothing has changed.

Nature is considered incidental.

That "primal knowledge of connection" the poet rhapsodized about won't magically instill itself in us on its own. It certainly won't make any difference in the world because we read about it here or elsewhere and agree that the environment matters, like that editor did.

Thoreau said that we are "made to love the pond and water." Love is a few degrees beyond recognition and most people aren't even there yet. We can't love from a distance. Well, we can, but only after we've met. Think about someone you love. You probably met them a few times. Yes, you can remember them fondly now and love them from a distance, but only after you've gotten to know them. How well do any of us know nature? How often have we met?

I am a diamond driller, searching for copper in a Vancouver Island rain forest. I'm twenty-one, bouncing along a dirt road in a pick up truck with my two colleagues, Big John and Dirty, Ugly Harry.

I venture a naïve comment about Indian ashrams and meditation. My friends react with explosive macho force, launching a hailstorm of obscenities.

I shut up fast but I know that I will remember this moment. "Hmn... there must be something to this."

Today, I'm fortunate to live in the Oregon woods. We have no immediate human neighbors but plenty of animal ones including deer, squirrels, owls, bears, foxes, raccoons, and skunks — not to mention the canopy of madrones, firs, and pines, thousands of plants, the stream and giant rocks, and trillions of insects.

We all live together in peace.

During the summer when our creek dries up, the deer drink from a circulating stream I built. When I meditate under the swaying trees where two waterways meet, squirrels and birds often come near, curious.

My wife and I hike almost every day along a maze of trails that meander through the forest. We aren't just getting exercise, we're visiting with our neighbors, paying attention, and loving the many species we share this special place with. We own nothing and they own nothing. We are not superior stewards; we are equal residents.

We belong here, together.

When I am communing with nature I am communing with God. The truth of God permeates the natural world, which is a revelation of God. I'm graduating from belief to nature-centered spirituality.

Real success ensures our species has a future — a future that many other species now threatened by our ignorant neglect and abuse might also live to enjoy — depends on humans regaining the ability to function synergistically within this revelation of God. That is the only thing that can end our abuse of the planet, other species, and each other. Period. This is the focus of leadership that quantum activists exemplify.

Most of us don't tend to harm ourselves, not deliberately at least. We abuse "others." When we realize there *are* no others, we stop hurting them because that would be hurting ourselves.

Real success means embracing our equality, accepting and celebrating that we belong in the web of life. We are not the single superior species exercising dominion over every other. These are our friends, not our slaves. Our success is interwoven with theirs. That's called "balance."

intelligence

Google gave me a list of the ten most intelligent animals, ranging from bees to whales. The author didn't put humans on the list. The next page was titled: 1,500 Butterfly Species Found in a Single Park. [8]

What do you think? Might we learn a few things if we paid attention to nature? Perhaps we might learn how nature thinks and how she speaks, not in words but with a meaning beyond translation.

Practice Two - Connection

"I am nature."

This simple practice involves walking in nature, consciously connecting with the Divine that lives there. As you walk, empty your mind. Let thoughts come and go, forcing nothing, grabbing nothing. I call these random thoughts "floaties." Let them float by and dissolve.

Our purpose is to transition from belief-centered to nature-centered spirituality. This is not pagan, it's pragmatic. As a felt experience, this practice brings a sense of intertwining, as one imagines roots connecting beneath the surface of the ground.

The feeling is of belonging and the image is any totem of your choice. You might connect with an animal, a tree, a stream, anything in nature.

The practice itself is simplicity itself: touch the earth. You can hug a tree, dip your hand into the stream, take off your shoes and burrow your naked toes into the soil. As you make tactile contact, utter the spell:

"I am nature."

☙

language

Nature is a language and every new fact
one learns is a new word;
but it is not a language taken to pieces
and dead in the dictionary,
but the language put together
into a most significant and universal sense.

I wish to learn this language
– not that I may know a new grammar,
but that I may read the great book
which is written in that tongue.

~ Ralph Waldo Emerson

I live in the forest. I meditate by a stream. I listen, intently, and am beginning to hear nature's song. She uses no words, but She communicates and it's possible to understand Her, even for a city boy like me. In a later chapter we explore how to improve your skills of eco-perception. That's an intriguing term.

Language *is* intriguing because words crystallize meaning in different ways for each of us. Consider the word "God." God means something different to all of us. I find the word difficult to use now, because it's become a weapon for the zealous, a cudgel for fear-based manipulation, even the patron saint for death squads. Millions have died defending their faith. That's the power of a word.

Many of our best words have been co-opted by propagandists. "Hope" once meant having faith that something better might happen. Now it means wishful thinking that we know won't produce real results. "Change" once promised improvement. Now we know it's just talk and things will stay mostly the same or even get worse. "Revolution" used to mean disruption, overturning governments, and taking back control. Now it describes a product improvement.

spelling

Like all books, this one is full of words. I use old words in new ways and have also invented a handful of new words. I already introduced "visionality," defined as "a future vision that becomes reality." More new words will appear throughout the pages ahead. Here are a few favorites that I use in mentoring sessions:

__Famory__: from "memory" – noun – meaning: "a future memory that feels familiar." Famories reside in the future. We develop famories as targets to aim towards and to reflect backwards from. Famories generate power in consciousness, they are magnetic by nature. They pull current reality towards them.

We can change the future with famories.

__Newmory__: from "memory" – noun – meaning "a new memory." I've coined the term newmory to describe a memory that has been visited by their owner who employed quantum activist skills to change it.

We can change the past with newmories.

We already time travel every day, all day long. We remember a conversation over lunch. We wonder about a flight to Chicago. It's just a part of our "normal" thinking. Time traveling proactively is different; it involves conscious intention. Streaming is the name I've assigned to a technique for doing this. We'll cover streaming in detail in PART TWO.

__Rigor frogis__: from "frog" and "rigor mortis" – noun – meaning "the point where procrastination on urgent change becomes irreversible." This references the well-known metaphor of a frog placed in warm water. He'll sit there while the temperature rises until he boils to death. He could jump out at any time but he doesn't because the temperature rise is too gradual for him to perceive an urgent threat.

Here are several of these new words used together: "I have a 2025 famory of my grandson celebrating the official end of the rigor frogis epidemic relative to acknowledging and addressing climate change."

How about this one? "I just created a newmory for that accident in '97. Turns out it was a real blessing in disguise." Note: this doesn't trivialize trauma. A consciously created "newmory" doesn't devalue deep, long, "inner" work. But it can give you control over something you had no control over originally. Now you do, reaching back from the future with a more mature state of consciousness. Because this isolated incident is now nested in the context of your whole life, it can become very different.

How we remember is important. So is our day dreaming. Words are powerful, how we speak to others and our self-talk. Language can keep us imprisoned or trigger transformation. Words are magic. That's why we call using them correctly "spelling." We live within the spell of words. But, as Walt Whitman wrote, "There are divine things more beautiful than words can tell."

more than words

Language *is* more than words and we're not the only species who communicates.

I visited the Damanhur community in Italy one recent summer. As I strolled down the corridor towards a ficus tree I heard heavenly music. Our guide told us we were listening to the plant.

> The Music of the Plants research began at Damanhur in 1976, when resident researchers created an instrument that was able to capture the electromagnetic variations of the surface of plant leaves and roots, and turn them into sounds. The desire for deep contact with nature has also inspired the 'Plant Concerts,' in which musicians perform while accompanied by melodies created by trees. The trees learn to control their electrical emissions, so they can modulate the notes, as if they are aware of the music they are producing. [1]

Our guide invited us to notice how the music changed as we approached and the plant adjusted to our presence. Stephen Harrod Buhner, one of my favorite authors, writes about our relationship with other species in *The Lost Language of Plants*.

The puppy looks up and sees you ... and his whole body begins to wag. 'It's you,' the puppy seems to be saying, 'it's you!' And in that moment something passes between you and the puppy. It is as if something leaves your body and enters the puppy, as if something leaves the puppy and enters you. And the most important thing then is to touch the puppy, to pet him, to hold him. And the puppy seems to want nothing more than these things as well – perhaps, in addition, to lick your hands or your face.

This is the experience that nearly all people know, yet we have no word for it in any language. (Love is too broad in its possible meanings, too overworked.) Once, people experienced this exchange with everything on Earth. The experience was understood, expected, a natural part of human life – this deep interaction with the nonhuman world – this exchange of soul essence. [2]

Any of us who have pets know this experience. But we may not know the depth of communication that's possible. Here's another example:

Chaser the border collie knows about 1,000 words, and if you believe a Duke researcher, she may be "the most scientifically important dog in over a century. But her skills aren't necessarily out of your dog's reach," writes Chaser's owner, John Pilley, in *Time*. "Any dog is potentially capable of reaching toddler-level cognition and development, including learning the basic elements of language."

Pilley taught Chaser through games, "speaking to her throughout the day in simple words and phrases just as I would to a toddler." Learning one concept led to another. For instance, at five months old, she achieved what researchers call 'one-to-one mapping,' recognition that a single word can refer to a single object. After that, she learned that words can be combined into different phrases, that one toy can have multiple names, and one name can refer to multiple similar objects (like the word stick.)

Her learned ability to follow instructions and to imitate matches toddlers' development, as does her understanding of pointing— something all dogs understand. Through play ... Chaser continued to learn things that were once thought to be possible only for humans, demonstrating that our minds and dogs' minds are much more alike than we think. [3]

the unconscious doesn't use words

Plants don't use words. Apparently they can sing, but we need special equipment to hear them. Your pets don't speak English, Italian, or Mandarin.

Neither does your unconscious. The unconscious communicates through images and feelings. Our culture emphasizes word language, but that's just how the conscious mind communicates.

Think of an apple. The skin represents the conscious mind. The rest is the unconscious. That image gives a sense of comparative scale.

Swiss psychiatrist Carl Jung said that we must "compensate the one-sidedness and narrowness of the conscious mind by deepening its knowledge of the unconscious." [4]

One way to do that is to begin noticing how we routinely use imagery. For instance, we might describe someone as a real "pain the neck." We might complain that we feel like we have "the weight of the whole world on our shoulders," or we might say, "Life's a beach." In fact, we employ images all day long, usually without being aware of it. If a picture is worth a thousand words, how much more is a multi-dimensional image worth?

Developing our abilities to stream through deep time into the past and the future requires learning how to communicate with our unconscious by proactively developing and employing imagery. For instance, I often ask a new client to tell me what an image for their life might be. Whatever image arises for them has wisdom to offer, sometimes leading to profound insights and clarity around impending decisions.

This is hardly a new idea for therapists and using imagery can be immensely practical. The other day I was wondering how best to heal a sudden rash on my feet. I silently asked for help and received two impressions. First, I thought of a local naturopathic doctor. Surely, I thought, she must have a homeopathic medicine for this. Secondly, the image of a wolf appeared in my mind's eye, big, strong, and aggressive. His silent message: "Dude, get on this. Take care of this situation right now."

I called my doctor friend who quickly diagnosed the problem and gave me a cream made from plant oils. It helped immediately and I avoided the need to attack my body with chemicals. Her cream contained a community of living beings intent on helping me, not toxic poisons meant to kill.

time is relative

Whenever something wonderful or traumatic happens, we're much more likely to remember. It can seem closer that something mundane that happened just yesterday. Fifteen years ago can be very near compared to whatever happened a few hours ago, when measured in degrees of emotional intensity.

We all know the feeling. "I remember that as if it just happened yesterday."

I use the term "deep time" to broaden our basic understanding of time. Deep time is holistic, not linear, and it is riven with wormholes, vortexes, and portals that can lead us backwards to memories and forwards to hopes or fears. We exceed the limits of linear time and enter deep time whenever we remember or daydream.

Time travel is a popular science fiction concept that usually requires elaborate machinery. In fact, we time travel every day in our minds. Our attention streams through consciousness ... never in a straight line. You will learn how to stream in PART TWO, to visit the future and seed a *famory* or to revisit the past and create a *newmory*.

Time travel movies often conjecture about whether we really can change the future when we visit the past. I say "Yes we can," but I encourage you to find out for yourself.

using new words

Begin working some of our new words into your conversations, at least with yourself. Start with the three we've already explained.

1. **Famory**: *A future memory that feels familiar.*

   - "That feels like a famory just waiting to happen."

   - "I need to work up a famory for that."

2. **Newmory**: *A memory remade with conscious intervention.*

   - "After creating that newmory I'm not afraid of heights anymore."

   - "It was an easy newmory to make and I've been able to forgive him now."

3. **Rigor frogis**: *The point where procrastination on urgent change becomes irreversible.*

   - "His mind is made up. I'd bet that rigor frogis has already set in."

   - "We've got a month, maybe two, to avoid rigor frogis.

————————————————

We are learning the language of wonder.

————————————————

಄

To see the world in a grain of sand
and heaven in a wild flower,
hold infinity in the palm of your hand
and eternity in an hour.

~William Blake

7

think

The world as we have created it
is a process of our thinking.
It cannot be changed
without changing our thinking.

~ Albert Einstein

If we take Einstein's radical proposal to heart, how will we create a new world with new thinking?

How about using that quality I've been identifying as essential for effective, transformative work in The Wonder Field? Can we "wonder" what new thinking might be like? Might it involve the heart, as well as the head?

Lynne McTaggart writes in *The Intention Experiment*: "To think is to affect. When we are consciously attempting to affect someone else with our thoughts, we may want to search our hearts about our true feelings to ensure that we are not sending tainted love." [1]

We can taint our thinking with ego-based conviction. That leads to manipulation, overt or subtle. It has nothing to do with wonder, which celebrates open discovery rather than fixed certainty.

the wonder of life

I began life drunk on wonder and never sobered up.

Wonder has always been my true north. It has survived childhood derision and grown stronger with every cynical attack, guiding my explorations of meaning and experimentation with friends and clients over decades, culminating in the "inventions" offered in this book.

> *I'm hiking in the Iao Valley on Maui. I pause by the cliff edge to survey the river below, the trees swaying on the far hillside.*
>
> *I feel that movement inside myself and close my eyes for a moment. The gentle breeze touches my skin and then drifts inside my body.*
>
> *The wonder of this moment merges with other moments, eternal in memory.*

"now" is a portal

Moments like this – and I know we've all had them – transcend separation. The veil thins and our "cut line" – that membrane between "me" and everything else – expands and thins. Oneness happens and it feels natural, like something we've just forgotten.

The more we learn how to sustain this sense of being one with, the more adept we become at conscious creating. This is the unique gift of being human I describe as "deep time activism." Our "being" exists in deep time, beyond linear time where our "doing" happens.

This has nothing to do with escaping reality.

In fact, the streaming process for traveling in deep time that you'll learn and master *expands* our experience of reality by putting "now" in perspective. Now is more than a point between before and later. As you'll discover through practice, "now" is our portal for quantum activism.

Speaking of now, if ever the single Chinese character that means crisis/opportunity was relevant, *now* seems to be the time. Doomsday prophets have always been around but never in such numbers, nor preaching "The end is near" with statistics grim enough to render hysteria credible.

Increasingly urgent conditions on planet Earth are compelling researchers like Guy McPherson to warn of a possibility that humans have never faced before: near-term extinction. [2] While there *is* a scientific consensus that human activity is contributing significantly to disruptive climate change, there is also a handful of outliers who disagree. [3]

What I know for sure is that we've had decades of missed opportunities to face obvious problems like pollution and deal with them head-on. Is it too late? Do our failures fatally doom us? We'll soon find out.

The important questions are these: Are we spectators watching an inevitable dystopian nightmare future develop, or are we activists who can change things? Can we, will we, take action to create a different future together? And, could action at a quantum level turn out to be our secret weapon?

Most people stay busy with alluring distractions. For example, an estimated 40 million Americans visit porn sites regularly. Meanwhile, our list of crises and problems grows. Most people ignore the signs, vaguely wishing for things to somehow get better.

I call that "lottery consciousness," as opposed to "semi-consciousness," which refers to the awareness of large trucks. Sorry, that's a bad joke.

New thinking confronts the risks. And new thinking strategies can *reduce* risks. Pulling that off would contradict our history, of course, which demonstrates that we *don't* learn from history. Actual threats are routinely denied and trivialized for as long as possible to preserve power and profit (think tobacco, lead, pesticides, etc.).

There are countless examples and here's a recent one: Exxon Mobile's own scientists verified the dangers of rising CO_2 emissions in 1978 and issued stern warnings at that time (that's almost forty years ago now).

The company, one of many who have succeeded by profitably liquidating our great grandchildren's future, buried the data and chose their own short-term greed over our collective long-term health and survival. [4] That's old thinking, which ravages the planet like a runaway virus. No variations on that theme will create a better world.

Those who expose and fight deceit like this are not treated well. "At least 185 land and environmental defenders, those who take peaceful action to protect natural resources, were killed in 2015, according to a new report released Monday. Those figures, the highest ever documented by the watchdog group Global Witness, represent a stark increase of nearly 60% from just a year earlier and an average death rate of more than three people per week." [5]

That's a shocking statistic for us, but it's a horrible reality for those directly involved. Imagine being murdered for protecting the earth. What sort of consciousness could pull the trigger and end a life over that? Old thinking justifies terrorism and murder in the name of profit. It's happening somewhere every minute of every day.

the wetiko virus

Old thinking is much more than some minor aberration. Native peoples identified an epidemic sickness of soul and spirit that the white man carried and transmitted. The Cree called it "Wetiko," a mind virus that has disconnected humans from each other and nature. Don Juan of the Carlos Castaneda books warned: "It has rendered us docile, helpless. If we want to protest, it suppresses our protest. If we want to act independently, it demands we don't do so."

> *Who falls prey to the Wetiko virus? Those humans who are not in touch with their own inner guidance, who project authority onto others and become part of an enslaved herd. There is now a full-blown epidemic on Earth. Thousands of brave truth-tellers have been marginalized, ridiculed, and even eliminated by those drugged to psychosis by Wetiko.*
>
> *"The Wetiko virus particularly flourishes in over-populated cities where people are "cooped up." As history shows us again and again, when we buy into group think and are enlisted as members of the herd, we become like cattle who are being raised by our leading psychopaths to be used in the service of their sinister agenda.* [6]

three questions

The Wetiko virus numbs us to the seriousness of our situation. It blinds us to the obvious need for united action now. How many lines have we crossed over the past decades, thresholds relative to pollution and climate change?

When it comes to predictions of disaster, Google seems to provide proof that scientists were wrong because not all their dire predictions materialized on schedule. [7]

Predicted catastrophes may not have occurred exactly as projected but they didn't go away and we face other, even worse crises now that yesterday's whistleblowers couldn't know about. Hysteria and denial are two sides of the same worthless coin. So, given all this, is it realistically possible to develop a common sense view of where we're at and, together, invent strategies that contribute to a better future?

We will have to think very differently, because what we've been doing so far — based on the way we usually think — is failing miserably. Years ago I asked myself three questions that I invite you to ask yourself:

1. "Do I care about helping to co-create a livable future for our great, great grandchildren?

2. "Am I ready to help right now?"

3. "Am I willing to embark on an adventure beyond the furthest edges of my ordinary reality, to explore and develop disruptive insights, to awaken from this civilized nightmare of disempowerment, and to be the change I wish to see in the world?"

If you answered "Yes, yes, and yes," you're followiing the right map.

the missing ingredient

Many who sincerely and honorably, even passionately strive to change the world for the better, continue to use old thinking and remain ignorant of quantum possibilities, as we've been exploring them. They believe that all we must do to get better results is to change our behaviors.

This explains the appeal of charismatic leaders who promise easy fixes for complex problems. Of course, their bold black and white pronouncements wither in the nuance of reality, but not before we sacrifice our sovereignty to follow them, sometimes even voting them into office. Then comes the disappointment and disillusionment.

What's missing from that "action equals results" equation is the medium of consciousness. Real and lasting results require changing not just *what* we do but *who* we are. And that relates to the profound difference between isolated human separation and synergistic cooperation with other species. If our ideas and action plans arise in a personal consciousness disconnected from the intelligence of the whole, they will fail to bring the change we intend *and* they will make things worse.

The road to hell will continue to be paved with good intentions until we walk it with a new identity and in a new direction, thinking differently, using our imaginations, and streaming through deep time to change the programming that's created this global mess.

living on purpose

It's one thing to be inspired, and I hope our learning adventure together is doing that for you. It's another thing to integrate inspiration into daily life and develop new habits of thinking and behaving. I've learned that it's neither an expert's brilliance nor the receptivity of a learner that determines the lasting value of a message. What makes the difference is practice. As Malcolm Gladwell wrote in *Outliers*, "...you need to have practiced, to have apprenticed, for 10,000 hours before you get good."

I call this "living on purpose."

In my mentoring work for individuals and organizations, I provide seven practices that clients customize for their personal and professional use. It *will* take practice over time to become adept at new thinking. Extending a loving influence via conscious intention and transmitting transformative impulses through our collective unconsciousness is what quantum activists do, expertly.

The "collective unconsciousness" is a term Swiss psychologist Carl Jung invented to describe the field of awareness that we humans share unconsciously. Effectiveness increases as we learn how to focus intention for deliberate impact.

This is the single most important skill any human can develop and the key to all our contributions. But, again, effectiveness depends on "who," not "what." What kind of person would adopt this as a priority?

Here's the good news: we're not starting from scratch.

I certainly didn't invent this movement. It's happening all over the world through scores of people who understand change must happen from the inside out. The path I'm traveling and recommending to you has been well travelled by millions who've preceded us. Thank you, pioneers, you've got more company now.

why bother ?

Here's the challenge: we've been programmed from birth and the Wetiko virus has taken a firm hold of all of us. This means that my proposal to change how we think might seem impossible, exhausting, and even pointless.

What good could it do, given the severity of our crises?

Consider again that lament: what *can* one person do? Remember that image I used, peeing in the ocean? Wetiko installs resignation. All of us are infected. Those who never learn how to neutralize the influence eventually succumb to discouragement. Why bother even trying?

As you can see, I'm not sugar-coating our dilemma. This is not an easy path but I'll take results over easy every day of the week and here are the results we are aiming for:

* ❖ A world for our great, great grandchildren to enjoy.

* ❖ A future that isn't a Mad Max wasteland.

* ❖ The experience of personal meaning and fulfillment, actualizing the potential we were born with.

* ❖ Experiencing that reward right now.

Is that enough motivation?

Actually no, it isn't. It has to get more personal. People don't donate to feed a million starving children; they donate to save Maria, one starving kid. They write checks for $27 and mail them in every month because it's something tangible they *can* do, not something noble they *should* do.

There's a comforting anonymity in mailing checks to a stranger. Kind as it is and a lifesaver for Maria, generous acts like this can prematurely satisfy our urge to help. What's really required runs much deeper.

Sending checks to save a starving child doesn't address why they are starving. It's because of the way we think, which determines the way we act. The "upstream" cause is what we must address.

Fact based climatologists have warned that human survival depends on fundamentally changing how we live on the planet. It's essential to be realistic, to face facts, and to act from knowledge, not delusion. But *how* we think about these things is all-important. And our positive-to-negative ratio is all-important. Remember the 80/20 rule.

the one-two punch

The one-two punch is a term that originated in the boxing ring. It's sometimes used to describe any successful strategy that combines opposite elements. For instance: good cop/bad cop.

When I operated my energy healing center in the eighties, we often convened seminars, sometimes in our own meeting room, but when we needed more space we would rent a public space. Sometimes the rooms we found were difficult to prepare.

The room reeks of smoke and stale beer. What happened in here last night? We've brought in plants and refreshments and music. Marcia turns up the stereo and a melodic flute fills the room. It sounds silly. I get an idea.

Someone finds a heavy metal cassette and we put that on. It's awful, jarring, disruptive. We turn it up full blast and escape to the parking lot where we can hear it blasting away through the open windows.

After about ten minutes we return to the room and shut it down. We put on the flute music again. It works this time. The atmosphere quickly shifts and we continue preparing for our meeting.

It took a one-two punch, first disrupting the pattern in the room, then creating the atmosphere we wanted.

ॐ

transformation

*... familiar forces are part of the unified field
that appears to bathe all of creation.
Because awareness of this field is so new,
scientists have yet to agree on a single name for it.
It's identified in research papers and books
by names ranging from the Quantum Hologram,
and Nature's Mind, to the Mind of God,
and often simply, the "Field."*

*Whatever we choose to call it,
this energy appears to be the living canvass
upon which the events of our lives are inscribed!*

~ Gregg Braden

This is the final chapter in PART ONE. We've been exploring The Wonder Field, my name for the energy Gregg Braden speaks of. I haven't attempted to exhaustively explain exactly what the field is as much as encourage you to use it. I'd prefer this to become your experience, not a theory to agree or disagree with or to be fascinated by.

There's plenty of science describing this field and many books I would recommend, including *The Intention Experiment* by Lynne McTaggart. Research away, but please start transmitting through the field right now.

Our intention is transformation and the field is our medium. If "transformation" seems overly dramatic, let's remember that we experience transformation every day. We take raw ingredients from the refrigerator, combine them, heat them up, and eat them. Whatever goes in our mouth is then further transformed inside our bodies, producing energy to build and waste to expel.

The ultimate transformation is death. None of us get out of here alive. We won't know what death is until we reach that final moment and make it all the way through the process. We're born, we live, we die. Then what?

> *Humanity seems to be approaching a crossroads, either the demise of our species or some kind of dramatic, transformative change. What will happen? Will we consciously participate in determining what happens? Will we live to find out?*

Humanity is under threat. The earth is not really in danger, *we* are, along with thousands of species we haven't yet annihilated with our ignorant and neglectful behaviors. Transformation – our own – represents our best and perhaps only hope.

But let's keep this personal. Forget the collective power of millions suddenly turning the tables. Forget any government action or brilliant CEO or benevolent aliens bringing sudden change. Hopefully, we've escaped the Drama Triangle by now and we're no longer identifying ourselves as victims hoping for rescue.

Change starts at home with each of us. But our efforts are not isolated. Whatever any individual does creates ripples in field and we are far more creative (and destructive) than we know. Because cause and effect are often separated in time and space, we don't always make the connection.

For instance, the Industrial Revolution brought us the marvel of pesticides. Yes, they helped increase crop yield, but it has taken decades to realize they are also damaging the environment and affecting our health adversely. We produce millions of pounds of toxic materials every year and residues even show up in newborn babies who test positive for over 200 industrial chemicals. Even in the remote Arctic. [1]

challenging illusion

This brings to mind an old episode from the original Star Trek TV series. Captain Kirk and a few of his crew were imprisoned a planet ruled by aliens proficient in mind control. I think it was Kirk who realized they were hypnotized. He began to strangle one of the aliens, who responded by transforming himself into an enraged gorilla.

This confirmed Kirk's insight so he kept up the pressure. As the alien weakened and his mind control abilities waned, we began to see holes in the walls. Those holes had been created by phaser blasts from the Enterprise crew when they had tried to defend themselves. Being hypnotized like Kirk, they didn't see the damage they did. They thought their phasers were malfunctioning but they weren't.

We're doing the same thing and, likewise, we don't see our damage. Someone cuts you off on the freeway and out comes the finger, while you press on the horn. I doubt that many of my readers would do that. But we might think it.

We might focus a dart of energy towards them. If that invisible energy could take shape in words it might be something like this: "You're an idiot. Get off the road. Get out of my way!" In *our* hypnosis, we don't see the holes our blasts create. And we sure don't routinely make the conscious connection between those few moments of concealed rage and a terrorist attack in Paris.

Paul Dirac wrote: "Pick a flower on earth and disturb the furthest star." Everything is connected and we are always impacting the field. Every thought, word, and action counts. So, why not focus loving intention for positive effect, knowing that those ripples touch everything?

Working in The Wonder Field as a quantum activist leverages this principle. If enough of us ordinary individuals change at a fundamental, causal level, to become functioning participants in the "trim tab," perhaps we can help nudge humanity away from the brink of whatever lies around the bend of denial.

Species come and species go. The question of the day for humans is: "Will we die in separation or transform in connection?" I choose to believe that our species is already transforming, gaining the same alchemical super powers that operate routinely in nature.

What if the scary situation we're navigating right now on Planet Earth is both an ending *and* a beginning? What if humanity is being reborn and these are labor pains? That sounds dramatic but transformation has happened regularly throughout human history. Human perspectives have shifted on a dime.

Imagine what happened when we realized that the earth was not flat but round. The flat earth assumption prevailed for many centuries as the accepted wisdom, until it suddenly didn't. Next came the realization that our earth was not the center of the universe. Wait, we're actually circling the sun in a solar system in a galaxy and its all moving in a universe that is expanding? That insight had significant psychological ramifications. Man is not at the center of anything. Just imagine how profoundly unsettling that must have been back then.

Today we're opening to another transformation of understanding. We may not be the only intelligent, self-aware species in the cosmos. In time, I safely predict, awareness that humans are just one of millions of other evolved species on many millions of planets will become the accepted wisdom.

Think about that. And think about how demeaning that idea is to our neighbors right here on earth. It's exciting to wonder about who might be out there in the starry heavens but what about whales and dolphins and cats and ravens. How do we prove that humans are so entirely superior? Certainly we don't rate high on intelligence in terms of self-care and management of our home environment.

Millions of us are waking up now, confronted by the possibility of species extinction - our own. Death will come for every one of us but, as Mel Gibson's character in the film *Braveheart* said, "Every man dies. But not every man really lives." It seems now that to truly live means to acknowledge the danger to humanity's survival and do whatever we can to help.

taking your transformational temperature

I thought I had always been fully committed to this work of human transformation, because I was born asking "Who am I, how did I get here, and why am I here?" But when I study my own lifeline and do some truth telling, it's clear that I've taken more than a few detours.

I haven't exactly blazed a straight path towards enlightenment, nor have I accomplished a mountain of social good. But you don't care that much about my life details and you shouldn't. It's your life that matters to you. So, let's establish a starting point right now to measure progress.

Take your transformational temperature. How eager and engaged are you with the personal process of transformation that I champion? One hundred would be nuclear hot, zero is dead. Before you volunteer a number, here are a few questions to guide you:

1. What kind of books do you read, what kind of movies do you watch?

2. What's your diet like? Why do you choose what you eat and drink?

3. What motivates your choices in friends, activities, etc.?

4. Do you consider yourself a consumer or a creator?

5. Do you have a mentor?

6. Do you maintain a daily spiritual practice, like meditation or yoga?

7. What positive social causes do you actively support?

Your honest answers to these questions determine your current transformational temperature. Having just read this list, invite a number to float into your awareness. What is that number, between zero and one hundred?

If it's sixty-eight, are you okay with that? Or are you embarrassed, as I was, surprised and humbled to realize that I may not be as devoted, as activated, as I thought? But what really matters is what I *do*, what we all *do*, day to day, — not what we believe. Behavior reveals our priorities and our lived values.

the transformational lifestyle

I'm advocating a transformative lifestyle because we'll be doing this for a while and there will never be one defined moment when we cross some sort of finish line. Change sneaks up on us, then, bang! The most radical change is death but I'm talking about living.

Who can speak of such a moment? Regular folks, I mean, not the Buddha or Christ. Transformation is usually incremental, a nudge here and a nudge there, plus those memorable epiphanies that brand us with their significance. It all adds up.

We've had moments. Some of them were explosive, others happened quietly in the background. I struggled to quit smoking for years. Then I read a book about health and became fascinated. Suddenly I was a non-smoker and friends were confused; "What do you mean you don't smoke? I've known you for years and you've always smoked." Not anymore. Five or six futile attempts riven with withdrawal agony hadn't prepared me for the ease of not quitting.

The difference this time? I didn't try to quite smoking; I committed myself passionately to being healthy. One day my priority was the pleasure of smoking; the next day it was the pleasure of being healthy.

All I ever felt since that day was better.

Smoking was a habit, and not a smart one. I have other bad habits and so do you. We all have our addictions. To live a transformational lifestyle is to change habits proactively, one at a time.

Can we really do this, when we probably struggle to stick with New Year's Resolutions for more than a few weeks? What will make the difference, what will help us persevere, for instance, with the practices you'll be invited to experiment with?

the difference maker

Here's an unlikely clue. Why can trees hold their limbs outward and upwards for years? Try extending your arms right now. How long can you manage? And how does it feel?

So, what's the difference between you and a tree? Yes, there are fundamental physical differences and the easy explanation relates to structure. But there's a metaphor here to inspire us.

The tree has roots. Those roots anchor it solid into the earth. The trunk extends upwards as do the branches, all connected to those roots, which balance the weight of what's above ground. The result? There's no effort involved in branches reaching towards the heavens.

To reach up without also dropping down invites toppling. A tree with shallow roots is easily blown over, no matter how large it grows. In fact, the bigger it is, the more likely it is to fall. For individual durability, our own roots must weave deep into the earth. This means being as alive in the dark as we are in the light, being fully human (our name derives from "humus" – the organic component of soil) and active in the human world.

The exceptions are some trees, like the mighty Redwood, that have shallow roots but connect underground with their neighbors. They literally hold each other up.

> *We strengthen our humanness by willingly traveling in the dark underworld, diving deep and linking with others in compassion for the suffering we all bear. This can exhaust us over time. It can drive us to discouragement and despair unless we also reach upwards for inspiration. Too much darkness or too much light — we must find the balance to enjoy a transformative life.*

We are called human beings. The human part is in our face every day; the being part takes deliberate effort to consciously experience in fullness. In this materialistic world, we don't hear much about being at all and a whole lot about doing. If we're interested in this "other," as you and I are, we must seek out help, from books like this, for instance.

grace

Direct experience of God is not meant to be a blessed rarity reserved for the sainted. We all have recollections of bliss and epiphanies in many forms. We may dream, meditate, pray or chant, sit with a monk, embrace our wives or husbands, read a poem, or watch a film. There are a thousand ways to experience the Divine, which lives in everything and everyone as grace.

Are you growing your relationship with the Divine? Are you going steady, are you married, separated, or recently divorced? Do you actually *have* a consciously acknowledged relationship with the Divine, or are those moments of random, unfocused, fleeting contact all there is? Casual encounters are not the best way to grow any relationship, hence my encouragement to adopt a regular spiritual practice. You'll be introduced to one in a later chapter, but I'm establishing this as one of two priorities before we venture into the practices.

The other priority is nature. Some of us are fortunate to live in nature. Urban dwellers need to be inventive. Buy a plant for your office, gaze out the window at nearby trees, take your lunch to the park.

The secret to accelerating our personal transformation is to deepen these two relationships. They actually turn out to be one, because the Divine lives in nature (and everything else).

In the film, *The Matrix*, Morpheus advised Neo that no one could tell him what the Matrix was, that he had to experience it for himself. Likewise, no one can tell you what a deep, loving relationship with the Divine is like, although I'm doing my best, just as Morpheus did for Neo.

You have to experience that relationship for yourself.

You've had your moments, we all have, and some moments have lasted long enough to compel you towards more. Some of us meditate every day. Some of us pray. Prayer gets results, that's been proven. But are they the right results?

I recall an apparently true story told by a mentor of mine years ago. A young boy became deathly ill. His mother petitioned her church and members began a prayer group for him. Miraculously, he recovered.

The boy grew up wild and eventually killed another woman's son. So, the question arises: should they have prayed for him to live or let him die? Now, there's a tough question which cannot really be answered.

It does serve to emphasize how primary our personal connection is with the Divine, so that we can know what to do that fits within the wisdom and appropriateness of the whole. That's why this material is in PART ONE and why it's called Tune In.

the vision board

Old habits die hard. Transformation is a new habit. It takes practice.

Daily practice is all-important because it takes repetition to install new habits. By the way, the common belief that it takes twenty-one days to learn a new habit is a popular misconception. [2] The average is sixty-six days and it takes from two to eight months of daily practice to integrate lasting change, to actually change our life experience.

I invite all my clients to get more conscious about their lives by mapping them all the way from birth to my target date of 2025. The vision board will be familiar to some of you, a first for others. Don't hurry to finish. Having a work in progress hanging on your wall is inspiring, especially when it tells the story of your life with images and poetic word spells.

Using images and words to tell the story of your life connects you with the influence of past choices. Looking back, you can better understand the implications of your decisions. You will also be able to detect themes and patterns, a design to your life that took shape according to your cooperation with, or resistance to the transformational impulse that has always been present in all of us.

Something is beating our hearts and steering the stars at the same time. And ... propelling us through life towards death.

Just because we are thirty or sixty doesn't mean we're all grown up. We continue to move through cycles of individual growth forever, as does humanity. Creating a vision board re-engages adults with their ongoing maturation process.

If we wonder where humanity is in terms of maturity, I think most parents would agree: we're teenagers. Humans, on the whole, are teenagers who think they know it all and don't clean up their rooms. We're ruled by our hormones and we make dangerous choices. Parents may wonder if and how their wild ones will ever survive into adulthood. We might wonder the same about humanity right now.

We might call our growing up "evolution" but using that word could provoke a distracting debate. Let's just call it life evolving itself in response to some kind of stimulation towards expansion and growth, a simultaneously organizing and transformative transmission that pulsates throughout the universe in what we call the quantum field.

A life line vision board helps your perception evolve. Looking back, you can learn lessons. Looking ahead, you can imagine the future you want. You can choose images from magazines and online resources, then paste them together with appropriate word strings on your board.

Having made these over the years I can attest to the remarkable value of seeing all this out of the corner of my eye, in an office or a bedroom, a visual reminder that this transformative impulse is at work in my life and that I am always choosing either to flow or resist.

Remember to represent your neighbors. You are kin with every other species, the millions and trillions that surround and fill you. Your body contains roughly the same number of bacterial cells as human ones. Imagine, you are teeming with microbial civilizations. We all are. [3]

We are not alone, even when we *are* alone.

building your life line vision board

Tape four sheets of 8½ x 11" paper together. Gather magazines, scissors and glue. Use a magic marker to draw a line from the exact middle of sheet two, bottom left, to the exact middle of sheet three, top right. Use your non-dominant hand and pause before you begin. Take a moment to close your eyes and tune into your life. Then flow. Make your line curved, with steps in it, dipping up and down, and include plateaus. Your intuition will guide your hand to replicate the story of your life on your vision board – past, present, and future.

The bottom left point represents your birth; the top right point marks May 1, 2025. Place a third point on the line to represent where you are now. Glue images and words that symbolize or visually represent the significant moments or themes of your life up until now in the far left area. To the far right, place visuals and words that symbolize the transformed state you are choosing and the future you prefer.

For instance, if you want to grow your confidence, the image of a roaring lion might become a touchstone reminder. A still pond conveys peace, a waterfall symbolizes power, a soaring eagle can represent freedom. As you choose, paste, and study these images, you'll begin to feel the transformative process I am describing. Look in the magazines for words like Breakthrough and Trust Your Gut and Go With It, Baby - you'll be amazed what you can find in magazines.

☙

two - turn on

Logic will get you from A to B.

Imagination will take you everywhere.

~ Albert Einstein

imagination

Let my spirit become a camel
And walk with its dark load into the wilderness;
And, in the wilderness, let it become a lion
Wrestling down and killing the dragon of false morality.
Then, O miracle, let the lion become the child
A dancing innocence and a holy Yes.

~ Friedrich Nietzsche

PART ONE was about tuning in and gathering information. PART TWO is about turning on and getting activated. The chapters will help you develop an imaginal tool kit for conscious transformation. Yes, we would like it all to happen overnight but that's not the way things work.

This is not a sprint; it's a marathon. It's a lifestyle — The Transformational Lifestyle.

shifting paradigms

"Space, the final frontier." That's how every episode of the cult favorite TV series Star Trek began. The full opening narration:

Space: the final frontier.
These are the voyages of the starship Enterprise.
Its five-year mission: to explore strange new worlds,
to seek out new life and new civilizations,
to boldly go where no man has gone before. [1]

I loved that mission statement. I loved that show. And I love re-defining space to reference inner experience: Inner space, the final frontier.

Inner space, consciousness, The Wonder Field. It's all living within us, ripe for exploration and discovery: new life, new civilizations, and going boldly where we have not gone before.

Here's how a client described what can happen when we pioneer in that realm:

"I felt fantastic. What I had envisioned for two weeks before was exactly what happened, the feeling was *exactly* the same. When my visioning met the actual event — one from the past and one from the future, together in the same moment – something really amazing happened. I was glowing. People came up to me and asked what was going on. It felt fantastic and it's changed me in some deep way."

clues

PART TWO is also a detective game and the clues begin now, one per chapter. The riddle will be solved in PART THREE, revealing my social change initiative and preparing you to create your own. Some of you may choose to join my project while many more of you will join others or develop your own.

> **Clue # 1:**
> *What is only real when you use it or don't have it?*

We may be allies in the trim tab but we can't all support the same cause. In fact, the more diverse we can be, the better, because we are confronting a host of crises that all need new thinking solutions.

think different ... to get different results

*Perhaps, I thought, intention was also like a star.
Once constructed, a thought radiated out like starlight,
affecting everything in its path.*

~ Lynne McTaggart

Here's a sneak preview of what's ahead in PART TWO.

10 - streaming

Streaming is our primary time traveling technique, meant to become an unconscious, automatic habit.

11 - famories

Step one of the Streaming process involves traveling into the future to create "a future memory that feels familiar." Famories work like a tractor beam, pulling your current reality forward towards your vision.

12 - newmories

Step two of the Streaming process involves traveling into the past to heal old memories and create new ones. You learn how to witness past events, especially traumatic incidents, and heal by supplying what was missing.

13 - story

You'll learn a radically different approach to the standard three-act story structure and how your life story is all an unfoldment of the second act.

14 - balance

We all need a first aid kit for communication emergencies. I call "and" the shortest and most effective mantra in the world, designed to rescue you from yourself or someone else overwhelmed by their own drama.

15 - see

You'll learn a five-step process for improving eco-perception, to see through the eyes of nature.

16 - life

We make choices all day every day. The more aware we become of their implications and learn to choose according to our visionary compass, the more successful we become at surfing the wave of fulfillment.

17 - death

Birth and death of the body are inevitable; life continues eternally. In this chapter you will visit your death and create a famory to draw you towards the ideal completion of your adventure in a human body.

18 - vision

In the third act, the hero or heroine returns home, bringing an elixir to heal the kingdom. This means that you *can* take it with you.

19 - stand

If we don't stand for something, we'll fall for anything. We will explore what it means to take a stand, "being" first.

20 - multitudes

Walt Whitman said, "I am large, I contain multitudes." We all contain a host of "selves" competing for center stage in our lives. You are not one; you are many, but the many are one. We will explore this paradox.

21 - imagery

We use images and emotion to grow a relationship between the conscious and unconscious mind.

There's your preview of coming attractions. Onward now, into the stream of activation and Practice Three which gives you the opportunity to focus intention in the quantum field every day.

the noon club

During the eighties, I encountered a program called The Noon Club. This was pre-internet and I can't find any mention of them online today. I'd be delighted if some reader put me in touch with the originators.

Their idea was simple: pause for a moment at noon every day to focus a prayer for peace. I did it for years and encouraged clients to join in. We connected with others around the world and experienced quantum companionship every day at noon. I've revived the practice.

I explain the potential impact by describing what occurs when soldiers cross a bridge. In the 1800's a suspension bridge in England collapsed when soldiers marched across it in four columns. Their synchronized marching set up a resonance that increased until it actually destroyed the structure. [8] The Tacoma Narrows bridge in Washington State toppled in 1940 when winds created the same kind of harmonic resonance. [9]

We use the Noon Club to set up a resonance in consciousness, to march in step and build harmonic resonance to the point where we can:

1. shatter those inner structures that sustain the infrastructure the Wetiko virus has built within human consciousness,

2. co-create new internal pathways to transmit value into the world.

ॐ

Practice Three – Imagination

What if?

Set your smart phone alarm to repeat at noon each day. When the alarm goes off, stop whatever you are doing. I like to stand, close my eyes, and silently voice a prayer.

I interrupt my busy day
to connect with the Great Spirit,
with my ancestors, my family, my friends,
and all living beings everywhere,
for a moment of shared unconditional love
and deep peace
honoring all that is sacred,
*knowing that **all** is sacred.*

As of this second book edition, I've changed my declaration. Now, I simply say:

This is the moment
and I am building the future
with love.

I stand in silence for another minute, feeling connected to everyone doing their own broadcast, wherever they are.

The purpose of this imagination practice is to begin working in The Wonder Field. Our spell is "What if?" and the motion is a popping sensation, like fireworks.

The feeling is child-like wonder.

The practice is as described above. Note: I've mentioned this to countless clients and friends and it seems the only ones who actually do it are those who program their smart phones on the spot. Later doesn't happen.

So, find your phone and program an alert for noon each day. I'll see you in The Wonder Field.

Spread the word.

10

streaming

Now more than ever we need to imagine our future,
to see the world we want to create.
This is what I call visioning.

The sea of change we are all living in also calls us
to ask some crucial questions:

"What's important?
What values do we need to embrace
and build into the future?
What kinds of organizations, institutions, communities,
and lives do we want to create together?"

People are struggling with these questions in all sectors of life:
in our families, work, communities, and governments.
Moreover, there seems to be a growing desire or need
to live on purpose–to be deliberate about how we shape and live
in organizations and communities.

"A whole level of accountability and responsibility
is therefore required.

~ Michelle Hunt

Streaming, as I named it, is a quick and easy four-step process for using imaginal perception to grow dreams into reality. What begins as an exercise that may take three to five minutes quickly becomes an automatic habit, easily accomplished in seconds and integrated into your life as unconscious competency. I employ layman terms to render this technique user friendly, but the underlying principles arise from science.

According to biologist Rupert Sheldrake:

> All living organisms show goal-directed development and behavior. Developing plants and animals are attracted toward developmental ends, and if their development is disrupted they can often reach the same end by a different pathway. In physics, goal-directed behavior is modeled in terms of attractors, as if future ends had an influence working 'backward' in time, and several quantum theorists have proposed that causal influences move from the future toward the past, as well as from the past toward the future. [1]

the four steps of streaming

1. Vision

"I wonder what it would be like if...?"

We begin by creating a famory (our future memory that feels familiar).

Pick something you want to change or create. You may have an event coming up. You may be planning a trip, finishing a project, or making a difficult decision. Start with something you can accomplish in a short period of time. Finding a cure for cancer or creating world peace are not good choices for this exercise. Choose something practical and urgent and finish the sentence: "I wonder what it would be like ...?" Examples:

1. "I wonder what it would be like to pay off that debt?"

2. "I wonder what it would be like if my marriage worked again?"

3. "I wonder what it would be like to get that promotion?"

4. "I wonder what it would be like if my event was fully subscribed and I sold thirty-five books?"

Here's an example of how Streaming works. I'll do this live as I write. And, to help you follow along, here's an easy way to unbundle the process into three steps:

Say it, see it, feel it.

My business partner Christoper and I have built an online learning game for leaders based on our book, Thriving in Business and Life. As of this writing we're approaching the pre-pre-launch moment so it's ideal timing for Streaming.

I ask myself: "I wonder what it would be like if our online corporate program launched with highly positive feedback and solid engagements for trainings?" I daydream, letting my thoughts roam to various outcomes, ideas, sensations. How would I feel if this happened? I would be thrilled, grateful, and delighted. I would feel hopeful that our skills building material to help executives develop and grow winning teams was getting out there, creating real value in lives and organizations.

Notice that I'm not telling a long story and that I get to the anticipated emotion right away.

Next, I pick a point in time when I imagine that these results are locked in. I choose the end of 2018. This gives me eight months from this moment.

Already, I feel motivated. It's tangible, it's beginning to feel real.

Now I *imagifi* the situation.

say it

First, I create a few words to describe the outcome I'm streaming towards. This takes some thought, some writing and editing, to come up with the succinct statement. I'll go offline for a few minutes right now to scribble away and then return with my vision statement.

"It's December 30, 2018. Our Thriving program is flourishing, with at 4 corporate trainings completed in 2018, 50 online programs sold, 4 coaches using our materials and solid inroads made with two government agencies."

I've evolved the system through trial and error, personally and via reported results from clients. I now believe it works best to name exact dates and numbers. I'll say more about this in a moment. The point? Be as precise as possible. This challenges you to think big *and* to be realistic at the same time. To say, "We'll make a million dollars this month" is not practical, unless you're already on the verge of that. So, be bold but pragmatic at the same time.

see it

The second step in the Streaming process is to visualize success and, contrary to what the term says, to use *all* your senses to see it, hear it, smell it, feel it, and taste it... if possible.

Why is this important?

Because you are creating a simulated experience to convince your unconscious that it's real. It won't be able to tell the difference when you create something that seems almost exactly the same. Since it's not yet in material form, your unconscious immediately sets to work to solve that disconnect by attracting the resources to create the envisioned reality.

Here's what I see: "I'm in my office boardroom with partner Christopher and a handful of colleagues. It's around 7 pm. I stand up and speak briefly about our success, addressing a sea of smiling faces. The room is warm and I can smell apple cider brewing. It's quiet, except of the faint sound of rain on the windows."

You see how detailed that is?

Final step: to feel it. It's vital to imagine that you *are* feeling it, not that you *will* feel it. So, you're there in your imagination, and you tune in to how you will feel, how you *do* feel.

In my example: "I feel proud and grateful, delighted with the reception our work has received. And I feel excited about the future."

Again, these are the three steps: say it, see it, feel it.

Clue # 2:
Those who have it can control those who don't.

your turn

I'm assuming you've picked your target. First, create your vision statement. Next, decide on a location. Remember the detail in my description. Use all your senses. Pick a location in the future when you have achieved your desired result and describe your imaginary location in detail. Where are you? Sitting at your desk, driving your car, standing by a stream, where?

Now, feel it. Ultimately, you want to create a feeling that's entirely distinct, a one-of-a-kind thing. *This* is the way it feels when you get *this* result. That's the only thing it could be; it could never be mistaken for anything else. You'll know when you get to that point because descriptive words will fail.

Example: how does cinnamon smell? How about spearmint? Describe your first kiss, the birth moment of a child. How about when your father died? You *can* use words but what you remember is multi-dimensional. It was what it was and it felt like it felt, period. This kind of one-of-a-kind specificity is what you are aiming for.

2. Truth

"This is the situation."

It's time to tell the truth.

If you are broke and walk around reciting, "I am rich," you are lying to yourself and ensuring future disappointment. You are *not* rich and your mind/heart/body/soul know it. So, that's self-deception. Besides, who would constantly tell themselves they were rich except someone who wasn't? Your subconscious will reject the lie and you will remain poor.

What *does* work is creating a vision of what you want *and* simultaneously being honest about the way things are. As F. Scott Fitzgerald wrote, "The test of a first-rate intelligence is the ability to hold two opposed ideas in the mind at the same time, and still retain the ability to function." [2]

You craft your vision in step one, now you tell the truth about the situation in step two. Back to my example, here's my truth: "We're just launching our new program. No one has bought it yet and we have no corporate commitments. Feedback has been positive but we don't know if people, companies, organizations, and government agencies will actually want to buy it and hire us. I feel nervous and a bit doubtful."

I'm truth telling here, simply facing the facts. This is *not* positive thinking, which journalist Barbara Ehrenreich warns us about: "... we cannot levitate ourselves into that blessed condition by wishing it. We need to brace ourselves for a struggle against terrifying obstacles, both of our own making and imposed by the natural world. And the first step is to recover from the mass delusion that is positive thinking." [3]

I agree, but that's not enough to produce change. Truth and vision must live together and that's rare. There is a third alternative between living in what she derides as delusional positive thinking (while denying a hard reality) and being preoccupied / depressed with what's wrong (while having no vision). We can learn to hold truth and vision at the same time.

Tell the truth about your current situation and how it feels. Be as honest as possible and resist authoring a long sob story. Just tell the truth, feel it, and move on.

3. Help

> *"Help! Help me please! Anyone... help me!"*

This can be hard.

Asking for help is especially hard for men because we're supposed to be tough like John Wayne and *never* need help. It's especially hard for women because you're supposed to be weak (so believe many men) and asking for help confirms it. It's especially hard for experts because they're not supposed to need help and admitting they do exposes them as frauds, or so the fear goes.

When I get to this stage in a coaching session and invite my client to ask for help, I often hear something like this: "It's true that I could use help with this. You know, it was easier last time when Fred was here but he's gone now and so I... well, there's always Nancy who, you know, likes me, but ..."

How compelling is that? Not!

Here's what I'm looking for: "Help! Help me, please help me. I can't do this on my own, I'm afraid of failing. I need help and I need it now. Please, please, please, is anyone out there? Hear me, answer me, help me now." This drops you down into a primal level, while the other was just a head trip. Which call for help is more likely to be heard? The squeaky wheel gets the grease.

Those who access ethereal realms are convinced we're all surrounded by angels who are restrained from helping us until we ask them to. Well, whether we believe that or not, why not ask?

It works like sonar or radar, transmitting a beam of energy that bounces off whatever is out there and returns to display images on a screen. Let's translate three elements of this process for our application:

1. **Transmission.** You ask for help. You send it "out there" into the void. There is a particular quality to your "ask." For instance, it might include desperation, urgency, vulnerability, etc.

2. **Response.** Your ask makes contact. It is "heard." The resources you need already exist, somewhere, but they are invisible and inaccessibly, until you ask. Just like radar, your transmission contacts whatever is "out there" and bounces back towards the screen of your conscious awareness.

3. **Reception.** You become aware of possibilities, inspired to think of specific kinds of help. Possibilities occur to you; sometimes you even get a visionary message.

A friend recently described how he overcame a sense of overwhelm by asking for help with a building project. He realized that he simply couldn't complete what he'd committed to do on his own, but this was a particularly skilled type of work that wasn't easy to hire for.

He decided to mention this in his on-line newsletter and immediately received a surprise response from an old friend, a fellow master builder. Long story short, 18 hours later, this friend was on site with tools in hand, having flown over 2,000 miles to help. Besides doing the work together, they renewed their friendship. My friend described this as a real break through for him, admitting that he couldn't do it all on his own and reaching out for support.

another word from our sponsors

Plants don't just yell for insect help when attacked — they also warn each other of impending doom. Strawberry, clover, and other ground plants grow by sending out "runners," horizontal stems that eventually bud into their own plants. These runners create simple communication networks between the connected plants. When one plant in a network is attacked by a bug, it sends out a warning to the network so that its siblings can build up defenses against the invaders, ranging from toxins to chemicals that simply taste really bad to herbivores. [4]

That's cooperation! So, let's take a moment to try out this principle. Focus on something in your life where you *do* need help. Ask, silently, feeling that request transmitting through your consciousness. Pause, ask again. Now, what comes back, what ideas occur to you? If you need help with a relationship you might think: "He's working so hard ... Hey, Ed offered to look after our dogs if we wanted to get away for the weekend. Why not?"

You might need help with a health challenge. You ask, admitting you have a problem and opening up for assistance. You remember something. "Didn't my wife mention a friend who got relief from a condition like mine? Right, I forgot. I'll ask her and see if whatever he did might help me too."

"Ask and ye shall receive," as the saying goes.

4. Action

"I act in harmony with all life."

Here's the final step that activates the full Streaming formula and delivers results: action.

All successful people will confirm that they had to work to get their results. The joke is: how many years does it take to become an overnight success? In the book *Outliers*, author Malcolm Gladwell says that "it takes roughly ten thousand hours of practice to achieve mastery in any field."

Sure, some folks get lucky. They know the right people and some are real geniuses, but here's what they all did: they acted. They did something and they kept on doing something until they succeeded. So, why bother with the first three steps then, why not just make the traditional "to do list" and get busy? If acting is what it's all about, why not just act? Because we need to know what to do, how to do it, who we are doing it with, and something to keep us motivated.

It's not enough to just act. It's not enough even to know how to act. That won't provide long term motivation. We need to know what the action is for, what our action is in service to, which is the compelling vision that we began this process with. Remember, that vision is pulling us now, working like a compass and helping us know how to navigate moment by moment.

Here in step four we are:

★   soaking in vision energy,

★   we've been honest about our predicament,

★   we've asked for help,

★   and now we make a commitment.

Whatever you commit to do must be simple. For instance, "I will build a new website" is a poor Streaming target. It's way too complex and it takes too long. Pick something easy and immediate. It could be: "I will call order that book." Or, "I will thank my husband for fixing that window."

Simple. Doable. Check!

living as if

Every effective technique has its key to success. For Streaming, it's living "as if." Once you have identified how it will feel to succeed, you commit to consistently experiencing that feeling now. For instance, with our corporate program, I identified how good it will feel when it's successful. Now, day after day, I live in that feeling, especially when we get a rejection.

I take all four steps. I keep visioning, truth telling, asking for help, and acting, over and over again, with this and many other goals. And, for every one of them, I'm having the emotional experience I want to have when we've succeeded ... right now.

when it works

We encounter a sudden, unexpected health tragedy. A hospital stay eats up our savings and we decide we must sell our house. Three other houses in our neighborhood have been on the market for many months and there have been no offers; asking prices have been slashed.

We begin using the Streaming process every day. We craft a vision statement that affirms our intention to sell the house for a certain amount (or more) before this date. We identify and begin embodying the feeling state we anticipate having when we sell the house.

About a week after the For Sale sign goes up, someone knocks on the door. It's a couple from California. They apologize for intruding and confess that something about the place has drawn them. We let them look around and they are captivated. They buy the house for list price.

What we imagined we would feel after selling the house and how it actually feels is exactly the same. And, interestingly, no other houses in our neighborhood sell over the next year, even with slashed prices.

when it doesn't work

I vision a Now or Never conference with colleagues. We pour months of brainstorming and thousands of dollars into planning the event and booking the room, building a website, etc.

Registration is very low. Team morale slips. One volunteer proposes a major change and a rift appears in the team. After mediation, she takes the conference in a different direction. The theme changes. I'm no longer involved.

My vision failed. But I keep going. I still feel how I imagined I'd feel after a successful event but this energy has been freed up from that event and I pour it into ... editing this book into a second edition.

And, I'm led into a vortex of inspiration. A whole new direction opens up as friends thousands of miles away call to initiate another event.

the slinky effect

Streaming may develop the physical result you want. It may not. But when your allegiance is to the feeling, the form can change and you still get what you want, namely the emotional reward of success. And something *will* manifest; it's inevitable.

A good example of how this works relates to the Slinky, that toy created back in the 1940's and still popular today. My favorite move was to place mine on the stairs and watch how the rear end caught up with the front.

It was inevitable.

It's just as inevitable that some kind of physical result will catch up with the vision you create for it.

You develop your future vision first – the front end of the Slinky. You begin experiencing the feeling state you want right now. Results – the back end of the Slinky – follow (as you take deliberate actions).

Will those results conform to your expectations? Probably not, because you can't control the universe. Results might be disappointing, they might be exhilarating, but you discover that the physical result is entirely secondary. You've created a target goal connected to a certain feeling state. You work towards your goal, using that feeling as your compass. You proceed, vision-first, feeling the reward of future fulfillment right now. And something unexpected happens.

Buckminster Fuller described this with a scientific term – *precession*. One online author defines it this way: "Think about honey bees. They spend their lives flying from flower to flower to collect nectar to make honey. They 'think' that's their purpose but their true (and much larger) purpose is to pollinate the flowers. This is the Law of Precession." [5]

One of his students wrote, "Bucky said that precessional effects are what most people label 'side effects.' i.e., I teach a person to fish so he can feed his family (Direct effect). One of his no longer hungry children now can focus in school and goes on to become an important scientist (precessional effect)." [5]

_____

The Streaming process is a powerful way to vision a specific future goal and create it. It's also a way to generate value on your way towards that achievement.

The unintended consequences of your vision-led actions may create results as valuable or even more valuable as successfully achieving your goal.

_____

࿇

*Don't be pushed around
by the fears in your mind.*

*Be led by the dreams
in your heart.*

~ Roy T. Bennett

famories

*The best way to predict the future
is to create it.*

~ Peter Drucker

Living backwards — living by accident — means *pushing* towards goals and waiting for results. Living forwards — living on purpose — means being *pulled* towards goals by a compelling vision and enjoying results immediately.

We predict our future and then we create it.

Clue # 3: *What do adults need but babies don't?*

the commander's intent

I learned about this concept from the 1994 business book by Jim Collins and Jerry Porras, *Built to Last*. They wrote about The Commander's Intent, a military concept taught in US Army schools. Wikipedia states: "The commander's intent succinctly describes what constitutes success for the operation. It includes the operation's purpose and the conditions that define the end state. It links the mission, concept of operations, and tasks to subordinate units." [1]

For instance, troops are instructed to take a hill, the one result they must achieve. But, as a Prussian general once said, "No plan survives contact with the enemy." No problem. The troops are given permission to change the plan in order to take the hill and achieve the Commander's Intent.

We must have a plan, but we have permission to change our plan, explained this way on a corporate website: "Even your business strategy and vision may need to evolve over time. But without a plan to guide you and your staff along the way, nothing will really happen." [2]

What motivates you to take your particular hill? Is it the promise of a future reward that keeps you pushing through, over, and around obstacles? Is it fear of the enemy or the threat of punishment for failing? Or, are you being pulled forward by a compelling vision motivated by present time enjoyment of the emotional "result?"

> *When you are living on purpose you decide what it will feel like on top of that hill. You imagine how you want to feel when you are standing there. You begin to feel that way now, on your way up. That's a very different kind of motivation.*

how famories work

Famories work like a magnet to propel you up those hills. It's never a struggle when you put vision first.

This is how you come to really *know* your goal. You feel it in advance. It lives in you. This transmits the frequency of what you are proactively and prematurely feeling. It establishes tension between what you are envisioning and the way things are. As long as you stay attuned to the feeling of your famory, you magnetize the development of a physical result to resolve that conflict.

I am conducting a marriage ceremony in a local hotel. There are about 250 guests and I don't know a single one of them.

Three days before, I'd received a frantic call from the hotel's catering manager. She knew I married people and reached out to me when the minister for this ceremony fell ill. I met with the couple and now here we are, with the bride coming down the aisle.

It's an odd moment. The crowd has been raucous and lively but now they turn somber. I begin speaking and a sense of dread fills me. I continue but the heavy feeling increases. Finally, I stop, put down my script, and speak spontaneously to the surprised crowd.

"I don't know you," I begin, "but I know that many of you are grieving recent losses." Two close relatives of the bride and groom had died in the last month and many of these people had attended both funerals.

"I appreciate that you've been through a lot," I continue, "but this is not a funeral. This is a wedding. It's a celebration. So, I invite you to give yourselves a standing ovation ... for having made it through the grief so you can be here today to share this joy."

After a moment of hesitation, they begin clambering to their feet until all 250 of them are standing, clapping, and laughing. I remember a grandmother swinging her cane in the air and grinning.

Then they sit down and I continue the ceremony, with a completely different feeling in the room. Afterwards, a number of the guests thank me for shifting the atmosphere.

Before we ever started, I did some Streaming to create a vision of what things would feel like – sublimely happy – and when I experienced the dissonance with how things actually felt, I changed my plan so that the emotional priority could prevail.

species intelligence update

Dolphins are not only the world's smartest animal after humans, they're so intelligent they deserve to be classed as "non-human persons." Scientists argue that their research on dolphins' brains shows it is unethical to keep such animals captive in amusement parks or to kill them for food or accidentally through fishing.

As reported in the *London Times*, "Recent studies suggest dolphins have individual personalities and a strong sense of self, and can think about the future. Bottlenose dolphins can also recognize themselves in a mirror and use it to inspect parts of their bodies, an ability I previously thought limited to humans and great apes. They can learn basic symbol-based language and adapt "cultural" behavior learned from other dolphins —all of which makes them likely more intelligent than chimpanzees, which are believed to be at about the intellectual level of a three-year-old child. [3]

---

*It takes perseverance and repetition over time to overcome
our default settings and establish new habits. Old habits die hard,
especially our tradition of pushing towards a future outcome.*

---

imaginal intelligence

Dr. Joe Dispenza wrote, "First, every day I would put all of my conscious attention on this intelligence within me and give it a plan, a template, a vision, with very specific orders..." Practicing this develops our imaginal muscles / intelligence. I remember Dr. Joe saying more about this in a lecture where he mentioned our habit of creating matter with matter, rather than energy.

That would be like giving a cow milk to make it produce more milk.

No, there's transformation involved. The future arises in our consciousness through attention and intention. Most people are thoroughly distracted and living accidentally. Living on purpose begins with acknowledging that we are the authors of our life story and that the future will unfold according to how we write the script.

As I mentioned, and I'll repeat this a few times, we cannot guarantee a future outcome, because we do not manage the universe. But we *can* make our plan and change our plan, course correcting our way to take the hill, to fulfill our Commander's Intent.

ॐ

newmories

*I learned that I never really know the true story
of my guests' lives, that I have to content myself
with knowing that when I'm interviewing somebody,
I'm getting a combination of fact and truth
and self-mythology and self-delusion
and selective memory and faulty memory."*

~ Terry Gross, host and executive producer of Fresh Air, NPR

We tend to forget what we choose not to remember. For instance, that fouling our planet with toxic waste is unhealthy. Here in the twenty-first century, not only are we suffocating Earth with our garbage (radioactive waste being the most lethal, CO_2 emissions and methane the most pervasive), we are also space littering.

"In over fifty years of space activity, 6,600 satellites have been launched with 3,600 remaining in orbit, and 1,000 of these are still active today." [1] This is from an online article called Experience Just How Much Space Junk is Floating Around, in One Astounding Interactive. Statistics are accurate to 2014 when they estimated there were over 6,000 tons of garbage floating around up there.

So, what might space junk symbolize in your life? Hint: what's floating around in *your* atmosphere? What litters your past? Do you hold any grudges? What memories torment you?

The past has become a haunted house for many of us. We can try to un-haunt the house through therapy and truth telling. That may help clean up the garbage but what about those who can't afford an expensive therapist? Of course, even expert counseling over years doesn't necessarily prevent the generation of more junk. There's another, easier, and infinitely more effective approach to dealing with the debris that floats around in our memory banks: turning memories into newmories.

streaming backwards

All of us have traumatic memories.

Over the years we may become aware how they are affecting our lives in negative ways. For instance, our father was less than kind and we suddenly notice ourselves being harsh towards our own son. Or, we were sexually abused thirty years ago and still shrink back from intimacy today, unable to freely receive and give love.

Here's a technique you can use on yourself to change your personal history by consciously healing memories with new thinking and imagination.

Begin by sitting quietly with your hands in your lap. Recall a traumatic incident from your past and imagine it resting lightly in your hands. Now turn it into an image, like a wounded bird.

Closing your eyes, feel yourself traveling back through time to visit that event. Notice yourself arriving as an observer, identifying with your future self, bringing a mature consciousness and perspective into this situation.

You ask: "What's happening here? And, what's missing from this memory?" If what's happening is cruel, then what's missing is compassion. If hate is present, tolerance and acceptance are absent. If anger is raging, there's obviously no peace.

First, feel how it felt back then. Relive the trauma but in the container of your more mature consciousness, as a guardian angel witness. I like to lead clients through this process so they feel supported but you can do it on your own. I do suggest beginning with something minor.

Next, identify and supply what's needed. Focus and flow the missing qualities you've identified into that memory. Stream love, forgiveness, appreciation, respect, compassion, empathy, understanding, whatever is missing. You are inoculating an old memory with the medicine it needs to heal. You are creating a "newmory," a new memory.

Obviously, deep trauma needs sustained attention and expert help. But this do-it-yourself technique is easy to master and, over time, it's remarkable what healing changes it can support.

I am twelve years old, sitting in science class, bored. I don't notice the teacher struggling to open a window blind.

His exasperated bark wakes me up: "Wilkinson, take an interest!" Embarrassed, the way twelve-year-old boys can so easily be, I leap to my feet and help him, feeling thoroughly ashamed.

Re-visiting this memory 50 years later, I realize my residual trauma has little to do with me or the window blind. Yes, the teacher is lashing out at me, but now – clearly – it's not about me. It's about him.

He's irritated, that's all. And I'm nearby. Something shifts. I feel relief and I send a wave of forgiveness into the memory, towards the teacher and towards myself, healing this old wound.

I just created a newmory.

Clue # 4:
What can't we live without
that can also sabotage our fulfillment?

species intelligence alert

According to a recent article online:

> The lovely scent of cut grass is the reek of plant anguish: When attacked, plants release airborne chemical compounds. Now scientists say plants can use these compounds almost like language, notifying nearby creatures that can 'rescue' them from insect attacks. A group of German scientists studying a wild tobacco plant noticed that the compounds it released, called green leaf volatiles or GLVs, were very specific. When the plants were infested by caterpillars, the plants released a distress GLV that attracted predatory bugs who like to eat the caterpillars in question." [2]

In science, the acceptance of new ideas follows
a predictable, four-stage sequence.
In stage one, skeptics confidently proclaim the idea is impossible
because it violates the laws of science.
This stage can last for years or for centuries,
depending on how much the idea challenges conventional wisdom.

In stage two, skeptics may reluctantly concede the idea is possible
but that it is not very interesting
and the claimed effects are extremely weak.

Stage three begins when the mainstream realizes
that not only is the idea important but that its effects
are much stronger and more pervasive
than previously imagined.

Stage four is achieved when the same critics
who previously disavowed any interest
in the idea begin to proclaim that they thought of it first.

Eventually, no one remembers that the idea
was once considered a dangerous heresy.

~ Dean Radin

13

story

Give me that holy wild laughter
That laughs at death and defeat and desolation!
I have seen my devil and he is profound and grave.
And in his gravity life shipwrecks and drowns.
Let the God in me rise like a dancer, and laugh.

~ Friedrich Nietzsche

Someone hired me to write a screenplay a few years ago. I learned the classic three-act structure and how this formula also shows up in the arc of a typical lifespan.

The first act is about disruption, leaving the familiar world to embark on a heroic quest. Equilibrium has been disturbed and the protagonist must now strive to establish a new balance.

The second act takes her into an underworld where she meets a mentor and undergoes training. She must grow and strengthen to prevail over challenges and actualize her heroic potential: kill a dragon, expose a conspiracy, shatter the glass ceiling, etc.

The third act marks her return. She brings back gifts earned in the underworld, some kind of "elixir" to renew the kingdom.

It's interesting to apply this three-act structure to our lives. An even more intriguing proposition is to wonder if all this that we call life is only the second act? Let's map out what that might mean.

Act One: Before birth. We exist in some dimension of love and light and meaning, forever mysterious and unfathomable to our conscious minds but sensed subconsciously and experienced as real to varying degrees by evolved spiritual masters down through the ages.

Act Two: Birth to death. Equilibrium is disturbed at birth. No wonder we cry! Whatever "before" was like, we can assume it was profoundly different than the world we're born into. "Underworld" is an apt description for it. So, we arrive. We live and learn, we build families, meet our enemies and friends and lovers, face challenges, give our gifts, and then we die.

Act Three: Beyond death. We return to that original dimension and, hopefully, we bring our gifts with us — to renew *that* world. Ironically, this would mean that we *can* take it with us.

Usually, if a person wonders about life after death (or life before birth) images of perfection arise. Angels float on clouds, etc. The suggestion that the after-life needs improvement or even healing and that we could help ... who's considered that?

Clue # 5:
*What is thinner than cardboard, invisible,
and more powerful than a drug?*

species intelligence report

It won't surprise most dog owners, but now scientists know it: The average dog is as smart as a two-year-old child," reports *The Telegraph*. Dogs understand up to 250 words and gestures, can count to five, and do basic calculations. "Obviously, you can't have a conversation with a dog"—at least not a two-way conversation—but dogs are among the most intelligent animals, and rival apes and parrots in language comprehension," says researcher Stanley Coren. "Border collies and retrievers were the breeds that scored the highest on tests usually used to measure young human abilities." Something else owners of 'bad dogs' know: Their tail-wagging pets can "deliberately deceive—which is something that young children only start developing later in their life," said Coren. [1]

about the second act

It's easy to make the case for life being the second act because this *is* an underworld, full challenges and threats. It's also a crazy place. We think of ourselves as rational beings but we're actually rationalizing beings when it comes to legitimizing the nuttiness of this human world.

Here's a joke that nails our hypocrisy and unexamined conceptual insanity: Two priests approach their bishop. "Can I smoke while I pray?" asks one. "Absolutely not," comes the stern reply. "Prayer is sacred." The second priest asks, "Can I pray while I smoke?" The bishop answers, "Yes. Prayer is sacred; you can pray any time."

> *Our beliefs blind us to the insanity of our behavior. My favorite proof relates to the sun. There it is, bright in the sky, the power source for our entire planet yet, somehow, we've managed to ignore it. Instead of learning how to use "solar power," the original and enduring fuel for the entire earth, we chose to burn hydrocarbons and pollute our air.*

Henry Ford popularized the internal combustion engine, which runs on this toxin. He said: "If you think you can, you can. If you think you can't, you can't." [2] He also said, "You must never, even for a second, let yourself think that you can fail. Our first principal is that failure is impossible. You may not get what you're trying to do right the first time or the second time or the tenth time or the 100th time, but if you shut out of your mind the possibility of being licked, then you are bound to win." [3]

There are a thousand success stories that prove Ford right, success that may just cost us our grandchildren's future.

Imagine Ford presenting this internal combustion powered car idea to his wife and her saying: "Are you nuts? It's stinky, noisy, and unhealthy. What about the sun? Couldn't you find a way to use sunlight for energy instead?"

There are many other examples of ignoring natural resources in favor of making our own. Add it all up and you get the toxic environment we've created where struggle and suffering seem inevitable. But if we know we are meant to take something with us – the harvest from our lives — we can strategize towards a better departure, which would include feeling proud of our legacy, that we have contributed to a healthy world for our great grandchildren to inherit.

Years ago I interviewed the man Ian Fleming based his James Bond stories on. Conrad and I met at his chalet in Colorado. He was pushing ninety at the time and I asked him about death. He lit up and said, "I'm in no hurry to leave. But when the time comes I'll have my bags packed and I'll be ready. I've always enjoyed traveling."

———————————————

The second act doesn't last forever.
Life in a human body will end.
We'll have to settle for eternity.

———————————————

ॐ

balance

I have been an explorer looking for new worlds,
not a harvester from safe
and productive fields, and life at the frontier
has shown me that there are no certainties
and that dogma is usually wrong.

I now recognize that with each discovery
the extent of the unknown grows larger, not smaller.
The discoveries I made came mostly from doubting conventional
wisdom, and I would advise any young scientist
looking for a new and fresh topic to research
to seek the flaw in anything claimed by the orthodox
to be certain.

~ James Lovelock

Remember the 1980 film, *Airplane?*

The protagonist, played by Robert Hays, drove several other passengers to suicide with unending narratives about his troubled life. I bet most of us have endured versions of this torture ourselves when confronted by someone who won't shut up about how terrible their life has been.

It often starts with an innocent question: "Hi, how's everything?" Usually you get something like, "Fine, how about you?" However, sometimes it goes more like this: "Not good. I lost my job yesterday and I'm broke. Man, my wife is freaking out and the kids are on drugs."

Here's a tactic that can save you hours of verbal waterboarding over the course of your lifetime: Interrupt. Interrupt him or her with a one-word question: "And?"

I do this frequently and it always stops them in their tracks. Eyebrows shoot up and eyes glaze over. "What?" It's called a "pattern interrupt," which some readers will recognize is a neuro linguistic programming technique used to quickly alter thought patterns and behaviors.

what's your vision ?

"What's your vision?" That's what I say next, to explain what "and" means. Now things get really interesting because virtually no one *has* a vision, at least not specific to the circumstance they've been over-describing.

Notice that the word is "and," not "but." Using "but" tends to invalidate what came before, for instance, "I love you *but* I'd like you to change." True love is unconditional so there's no "but." The word "and" plays differently. "And" acknowledges the value of what came before. "I love you *and* I'd like to discuss some ideas for changes."

Every situation in life has an "and." One side is the way things are, the other side is the way you want them to be. "And" is the edge. "And" leads to balance.

And also applies to the way we create our lives. Some people are addicted to magical thinking, expecting miracles to land on their laps while they meditate or watch TV. Others are bulldogs who believe that hard work is the road to success. "And" is a way to travel both paths.

After seven months in Ashland, Oregon we are ready to buy a house. My wife scours the papers, circling possibilities, making over forty phone calls, enlisting realtors, and touring homes for sale. One day, she shows me an ad. I barely read it before feeling and saying: "This is the one." We immediately drive to the address. At that same moment, a car pulls up in the neighbors driveway; it's our realtor. She lives next door!

We are able to look inside and decide we want the home. Our offer is submitted before other realtors tour the property so we avoid a possible bidding war. When friends visit and applaud our magical find I remind them that it was more than luck or fate. My wife did the hard work. Usually, both are necessary.

And ...

and ...

the secret ... not !

I'm a cautious fan of Barbara Ehrenreich's expose on delusional optimism: *Bright–Sided, How the Relentless Promotion of Positive Thinking Has Undermined America.* She describes this country's epidemic of optimism as a formula for escaping reality.

She also slams *The Secret*, a 2006 documentary film that went viral. The Wiki entry describes it's message this way: "... everything one wants or needs can be satisfied by believing in an outcome, repeatedly thinking about it, and maintaining positive emotional states to 'attract' the desired outcome." [1]

I remember watching *The Secret* with friends, increasingly nauseated by the silly fluff parroted by one spiritual entrepreneur after another. Feel-good phrases abounded, reminiscent of what Napoleon Hill wrote in his book *Think and Grow Rich* and Henry Ford's maxim, "If you think you can do a thing or think you can't do a thing, you're right." What about diligence and sustained work?

There's no "and" here.

All we need to do, apparently, is to believe we are wealthy, repeat some positive mantras, and then welcome in the abundance that surrounds us and magically converts into money and expensive stuff.

If the formula fails to work, that's due to limitations in our thinking, our "scarcity consciousness." To break through, we only need to remain relentlessly optimistic, to "believe our way to riches and success and happiness and spiritual enlightenment.

This nonsense monetizes spiritual principles for greedy gain and is championed by those who should know better. The idea that "thoughts become things" is not an immutable, inevitable, eternal law in every instance. "I can fly, I can fly, I can fly" doesn't work. I'm not going to prove that by jumping off a bridge.

Here's who the formula *does* work for: self help gurus.

Clue # 6:
What is both ancient and modern and often causes problems?

more from nature

Certainly plants don't 'remember' the way humans do, but a group of researchers discovered that plants learn to associate various wavelengths of light with different kinds of danger. Scientists would shine light on plants for an hour, then expose them to a virus. This was a pathogen the plants could protect themselves from by manufacturing a particular chemical. What the scientists discovered was that the next time they shone light on the plants for an hour, its leaves began to manufacture the chemical necessary to fight the virus. It didn't manufacture the chemical at other times — only when exposed to the same kind of light for the same amount of time. The scientists speculated that perhaps plants have developed this 'memory' because each season brings with it a change in the light — as well as changes in the kinds of pathogens likely to attack the plants. So from an evolutionary perspective, a plant that learns to associate light duration with certain pests is going to survive longer." [2]

both sides of the coin

As much as I admire Ehrenreich's much-needed and long overdue takedown of the positive thinking movement — and I don't doubt her compassionate intentions — in the end she cheats us of a balanced understanding.

Yes, ungrounded optimism based in denial of hard facts results in delusional ruination. It's just a matter of time before those dream castles fall. I share her deep concern for the millions who have been hoodwinked by this philosophy and suffer because of it. And... our thoughts *do* make a difference.

In fact, as you are discovering in this book, vision is vital, *if* we are going to solve our problems with new thinking. Ehrenreich champions practicality on its own which, I believe, is insufficient.

She concludes her book this way:

> Happiness is not, of course, guaranteed, even to those who are affluent, successful, and well loved. But that happiness is not the inevitable outcome of happy circumstances does not mean we

can find it by journeying inward to revise our thoughts and feelings. The threats we face are real and can be vanquished only by shaking off self-absorption and taking action in the world. Build up the levees, get food to the hungry, find the cure, strengthen the 'first responders!" We will not succeed at all these things, certainly not all at once, but – if I may end with my own personal secret of happiness – we can have a good time trying. [3]

Here is what I disagree with: "The threats we face are real and can be vanquished only by shaking off self-absorption and taking action in the world." Is that the "only" way? What is creating these threats upstream?" A certain kind of thinking. That's the deeper cause.

What's the long-term result of ignoring causes to wrestle with effects downstream? Precisely what we are experiencing on the planet right now. Without vision, we just flail around with good intentions. Actions have their essential place but they are never enough on their own. A bird with one wing flies in circles.

Notice how much time you spend worrying about a problem vs. how much time you devote to developing a vision for the solution. I'm referring to your inner dialogue, the thoughts that stream constantly in that conversation you have with yourself.

Mark Twain famously said, "I am an old man and have known a great many troubles, but most of them never happened." We too may have rehearsed anticipated disasters in our heads many times, then we might talk about them and invite a listener to support our delusion.

"And" shifts focus. "And" invites us to consider the other side – positive or negative. "And" opens possibilities to adapt the way nature does. Of course, nature has an advantage: no committees!

---

new thinking ... a test

Years ago I heard a story about a college student who received a failing grade for his answer to this test question: "How do you determine the height of a tall building using a barometer?" I loved his answer.

"Take the barometer to the top of the building. Tie a string to it and lower it to the ground. Measure the string. That's the height of the building."

His professor argued that this didn't really utilize the barometer in the way the question required. But the student objected to this kind of narrow thinking and convinced his prof to consider several other "and" solutions he had.

"Measure the barometer's shadow on the street. Measure it again on top of the building. The difference will help you determine the answer."

And, my favorite: "Find the superintendent and say: 'If you tell me the height of this building, I'll give you a barometer!'" The professor relented and gave his student a passing grade for ingenuity.

There is *always* an "and."

trumping trump

Since the first edition of this book was published, Donald Trump has assumed the office of President of the United States, which proves that anyone can become president (as long as they are a game show TV personality, have unlimited financial resources, benefit from foreign election meddling, and leverage social media plus Fox News and hate radio.

Millions of reeling liberals are losing sleep wondering what to do about Trump?

The riddle is easily solved by examining his name. Trump was once Drumpf. An ancestor changed the name. Probably a smart branding change. So, what does "trump" mean? Miriam Webster defines the word this way: "a decisive overriding factor or final resource."

We often use the word to describe a strategy that can best any other. To "trump" something or someone means to get the better of them. So, why not trump Trump?

He's a divisive force, no doubt about that. Faced with the kind of intense polarization he provokes, the temptation beckons to get sucked into that game, to counter his extreme positions with your own, probably opposite ones. That creates conflict. Instead, use "and" to disrupt the game.

"And" doesn't dispute anything. Note the difference between these two statements:

"I love you <u>but</u> sometimes you really bug me."

or

"I love you <u>and</u> sometimes you really bug me."

"But" invalidates what came before; "and" simply adds new information.

trade positions for interests

I've been invited to join a small group of businessmen for two days at a remote fishing lodge. It only takes a few minutes to realize that I'm the odd duck of this group.

As we begin to converse, firm positions emerge. All these guys think very differently than I do.

I make a choice to use "and," not "but." I ask questions, I learn more about them, and we become friends.

This demonstrates another powerful use of "and," to ask questions and discover why someone believes what they just said. They have a position; so do you. But you can keep your position to yourself and find out what they are interested in that makes them believe what they believe. Try it.

And ...

૱

The best thing for being sad," replied Merlin,
"is to learn something. That is the only thing that never fails.
You may grow old and trembling in your anatomies,
you may lie awake at night listening to the disorder of your veins...
You may see the world around you devastated by evil lunatics,
or know your honor trampled in the sewers of baser minds.

There is only one thing for it then—to learn.
Learn why the world wags and what wags it.
That is the only thing which the mind can never exhaust,
never alienate, never be tortured by, never fear or distrust,
and never dream of regretting.

Learning is the thing for you.

~ T. H. White

15

see

... if nature is outside us, we trim its offending branches,
dam its rivers, level its forests.

But if we have an intimate relationship with nature,
we will seek to heal and humanize,
not simply manage it as a resource
to which we think we are superior.

This redefining of the self meets
powerful resistance in our culture,
where the self is institutionalized as a fortress
against nature. We need what Joanna Macy aptly called
a greening of the self.

~ Tom Hayden

Rachel Carson wrote: "In nature nothing exists alone." James Hillman spoke to how perception changes behavior. "See different, do different."

We're *made* of nature, we're *in* it from birth to death. Yet, we've separated ourselves to craft this artificial human world that operates in fundamentally different ways and we're destroying nature in the process.

We've actually ignored nature to the point where our poisoning of the natural environment could precipitate our own extinction. We can't kill nature, we can only wound her. Nature adapts, much faster than we do. Might we learn something from seeing nature differently?

Clue # 7:
What do we exchange with each other every day
that evokes strong emotional responses?

nature intelligence report

We may have to stop mocking gardeners who talk to their plants: University of Western Australia biologist Monica Gagliano found that corn plants could emit and respond to sound. Gagliano noticed that the roots of corn plants made clicking noises at around 220 Hz. She and her collaborators then grew corn suspended in water and played an artificially generated, continuous noise at 220 Hz. The roots responded to the noise by leaning towards the source of the sound. It's not clear why plants would evolve the ability to hear and emit sound, but Gagliano and her colleagues are trying to find out by gathering more data. [1]

Having scorned nature, we now approach a perilous crossroads. Woody Allen addressed our choices in his 1979 "My Speech To the Graduates:

More than at any other time in history, mankind faces a crossroads. One path leads to despair and utter hopelessness. The other, to total extinction. Let us pray we have the wisdom to choose correctly. I speak, by the way, not with any sense of futility, but with a panicky conviction of the absolute meaninglessness of existence which could easily be misinterpreted as pessimism. [2]

That's funny enough that I've remembered it for thirty years. But it's the kind of humor that hurts, because it strikes so close to home. We *are* a stubborn species and we've run out of good choices in the twenty-first century. And – there's that word again – this is a double-edged sword, because our weakness is also our strength.

Under pressure, during emergencies, we tend to pull together. But it has to be a *real* emergency, not just the description of one. The standard motivational strategy of "tell and agree" doesn't compel us into action, even when experts scream at us about an impending emergency. It's still theoretical until it happens to us. This underlines the necessity of learning how to make our visions real. Let's start in the woods.

nature first

Laura Sewall is a perceptual psychologist and the author of *Sight and Sensibility*, as well as an essay called *The Skill of Ecological Perception*.

In her essay, which appears in the book, *Ecopsychology, Restoring the Earth, Healing the Mind*, she details five perceptual practices that can help us "come to our senses."

1. Learning to Attend

Sewall details the distinction between "endogenous" and "exogenous" attention. Endogenous attention is "perceptual readiness." She describes this as "...the largely unconscious placement of one's focus on internal desires, needs, and priorities. It acts as a filter or gate, selecting particular information from the visual field... When I am hungry, restaurant signs 'pop out' of any long row of commercial buildings." [3]

I call this The "Subaru Effect." If you are shopping for a Subaru you will start to see them everywhere. Where did they all suddenly come from? They were always there but your conscious interest triggered a subconscious selection, which now gives them preferential value in your unconscious visual choices.

Anyone who's tripped on LSD knows what happens when our perception filters are temporarily suppressed. The data assault can be overwhelming. There's so much information coming in at the same time that every day functions like driving become impossible. Visual filtering is necessary to function effectively. What we filter for is the question.

"By filtering the visual world consistent with previous experience or mental states, endogenous attention builds and perpetuates one's view of reality." [4] In other words, our view of reality – which is *not* reality, just our view of it – sustains what we believe to be true.

I'm ten, helping my father build a carport. He asks me to go into the garage and bring back the finishing nails. I shudder, already knowing from past experience, that I won't be able to find them. Sure enough, I search and search — there are no nails to be found.

I report my failure and Dad shakes his head wearily.

He leads me back to the garage and points. Miraculously, there are the nails, right on the workbench where he said they would be... but I couldn't see them.

Exogenous attention is about focus, seeing the details of what is actually present. Sewall explains: "To develop this ability, one must nurture a receptive stance and a sensitivity to spatial and temporal changes within the landscape. This particular form of attention seems to be most susceptible to psychic numbing; when numb, we notice as little as possible. Thus, intentionally nurturing this form of awareness requires getting out of one's head; it is opening one's self." [5] There is no substitute for nature. Un-numbing can happen as we walk in the woods.

I'm laboring through the second day of a planned four-day solo Vision Fast near Death Valley. It's ninety-five degrees and I've foolishly exhausted myself building a rock retaining wall to level a sleeping space within a steep crevice. I try water, salt, meditation and prayer, but nothing helps settle my pounding heart and escalating dizziness.

I begin breathing rhythmically and survey the rocky terrain. Something catches my attention, just a feeling first and then I see it. There's some breed of squirrel between two rocks nearby, staring at me intently. I tune in and hold each others gaze.

He is not afraid. We are both curious. A communication of some kind happens and I feel a shift in my body. My physical stability returns.

regaining the sense of belonging

Find a trail and pause before you cross that threshold from the parking lot into nature, anticipating the impending shift. Take that last step and notice how it feels. Acknowledge your default setting of separation as the way things used to be. The way things are becoming – because you are choosing it — is a profound and primordial sense of belonging.

Now walk, unhurried and relaxed, focusing your attention softly and fully on where you are and who you're with. This accesses your exogenous attention, "the way in which our gaze is drawn to novelty or change within the visual field." [6]

Nature is always close and she also lives within us. As Stephen Harrod Buhner wrote in *Plant Intelligence and The Imaginal Realm*: "James Lovelock ... noted that 'Gaia is an emergent phenomenon, comprehensible intuitively, but difficult or impossible to analyze by reduction.' To sense the pattern that connects us, and to then use it to travel deep into the heart of the natural world, you have to have, at the root of your approach, the capacity for *feeling*. You can't get there through thinking alone. It's feeling first, thinking after." [7]

2. Perceiving the Relations

Commit to spending time with your new lover every day.

That's how we grow any relationship. Sewall writes about our materialistic society and how we are programmed to perceive objects, not relationships. "One way to make this shift from perceiving objects to perceiving context or relations is to observe the interface between water and land." [8]

My wife and I walk in our Oregon forest almost every day. Although we often follow the same trails, they are always new. Several streams flow through our property and they change daily. The sun is always filtering through the leaves and branches in unique patterns, illuminating the ripples of water spraying on mossy rocks. I walk within this symphony and all my senses light up. Sometimes I recall the Lakota prayer, *Mitákuye Oyás'iŋ:* "all my relations."

3. Perceptual Flexibility

Most of us have played with 3D posters that conceal a second image, only visible when we shift our gaze. Remember how that moment of softening to see the hidden image? That's what Sewall describes at this stage.

Rachel Carson wrote, "Those who contemplate the beauty of the earth find reserves of strength that will endure as long as life lasts. There is something infinitely healing in the repeated refrains of nature — the assurance that dawn comes after night, and spring after winter." [9] Again, these words are useless unless we enter nature for a real life experience. Experience leads to changed behavior. "See different, do different."

Sewall advises: "It requires a fluidity of mind in which the magic of the visible world is revealed by relinquishing one's expectations and nurturing a freshness of vision. It is seeing familiar patterns within apparent chaos, rearranging the pieces and allowing a new image to emerge." [10]

I am walking alone through our forest on a warm summer day. I feel lazy, tired, content. I pause to sit on a rock. My eyes flutter closed, open again, I notice the scenery shifting and blurring.

I am "seeing" differently. It's difficult to describe because so much of the change is emotional. I "feel" nature.

4. Re-perceiving Depth

Can you recall walking through the bottom of a deep canyon? This is one way to regain a sense of living *in* the earth, not *on* it.

Sewall describes the phenomenon this way: "The recognition of *being within* carries with it a number of psychological repercussions. Quite noticeably, a sense of being within produces a distinct vulnerability; it is a recognition of one's psychological permeability and lack of control. But there is also a kind of ecstatic liberation, a freeing from the need to control. One feels a relinquishing of defenses and separation, and with it a mysterious sensuality." [11]

This is an experience of oneness with that can arrive in any unguarded moment to un-numb us. Solo time in nature can drop us deep within nature's womb. From this place of connection we may wonder why we would ever behave in ways that harm ourselves.

5. The Imaginal Self

Sewall completes her instructions with a warning about how the assault of sensory overload has atrophied our imaginations. Fortunately, we can regain that capacity.

> With practice, one's ability to imagine becomes colorful, vivid, creative, and emotionally provocative, thus enriching and influencing our psychological experience. With practice, we can develop clear visions, images for our children and for the future, to which we will be devoted. These visions are the images to nurture and feed with psychological energy. They are the images that may guide our daily, unconscious choices. They are the images that will serve to create the world in which we wish to live. [12]

Learn to see with the eyes of nature, to experience walking *in* the earth, not *on* the earth. We can see different and do different.

That's new thinking. That's eco-perception in action, and that's the foundation we take into all our visioning work.

҂

Practice Four - Balancing

"And ..."

The purpose of this practice is to use "and," the designated spell, as a pattern interrupt for creating balance.

You can use it on yourself, to shift negative self-talk. You can use it in conversations, finishing something you are saying with that word ... just leaving it hanging as an invitation to another viewpoint. I have a friend who says, "Or not" after he finishes an impassioned rave.

The movement is back and forth. The feeling is flexibility or resiliency and the image is a pendulum.

The practice, like the spell, is profoundly simple. Just shift your physical body. We all tend to get stuck, in a physical position or a mental one. So, whenever you want to use this practice, just move. It can be slight – adjusting your position in the chair. It can be more dramatic – standing up and walking around.

"And" is a magic word. It can shift things immediately. Moving your body is a magic remedy for dealing with stagnation. It's profoundly simple, but powerful.

Life is never made unbearable
by circumstances,
but only by lack of meaning and purpose.

~ Victor Frankl

life

Life is a series of natural and spontaneous changes.
Don't resist them — that only creates sorrow.
Let reality be reality.
Let things flow naturally forward
in whatever way they like.

~ Lao Tzu

We can use imagination to escape our current reality or to create a new one. We can manipulate the external world to get more toys and short-term pleasure or we can produce value, meaning, and long-term fulfillment. Looking at it that way you'd think this would be an easy choice. Actually, it's not.

Why not? Because we've been educated/programmed for preoccupation with external superficiality. That superficiality includes immediate gratification — whatever feels good in the moment — and society supports our addictions. Mother may have said, "Eat your vegetables" but most of us prefer sugar. And how many doctors advise us differently?

Clue # 8:
Some say it's over-rated
but that's because they have plenty of it.

Ideally, we would be educated to choose well, to know what decisions to make moment by moment to develop a fulfilling experience, contribute to the well being of neighbors, and enhance our home environment.

How do you think plants know when to flower? That's right — they're keeping track of time. Scientists have recently identified a set of proteins in plants that respond to the amount of light they're exposed to during the day. When they receive enough light per twenty-four-hour period, these proteins send a signal that activates the flowering cycle. [1]

Through open-hearted exposure to *that* intelligence, we can revive our instinctual awareness of how to act in harmony with all other species, starting with each other. We can make our choices with everyone in mind, not just ourselves.

a formula for life

It's never too late to program yourself to live differently. I've refined this into four components: face forward, keep practicing, be accountable, and get going. Each can be used on their own.

1. Vision

We've already described the role that vision plays in the Streaming process, but let's emphasize how incredibly significant visualization is, even on its own.

There's a verse from Proverbs in the Bible: "Where there is no vision the people perish." There's a lot of perishing going on in the twenty-first century. Real vision is conspicuous by its absence in every area of life. Individuals, with no destination in mind, wander aimlessly with other confused, meandering lost souls.

Vision is meant to be an integral part of our lives, not something we record on a flip chart. What *is* your vision for your life and for the world? Is vision an integral part of your life, something that you consciously employ every day?

Consider this: What would driving be like if you kept your eyes glued to the rear view mirror? Don't you look through the windshield when you drive? Why? Because it's important to know where you're going. If you don't, you crash. This explains why we crash in life. We're transfixed by our past, constantly revisiting what happened back then.

Or, we're preoccupied with the immediate challenges of the present. This would be like constantly looking around the interior of our car. It's okay to glance around, and we have a rear view mirror for good reason, but the windshield rightly claims ninety-five percent of our attention. Imagine if we did the same in life, if we actually lived vision-first by facing forward.

2. Practice

You know the joke about someone in New York asking for directions: "How do I get to Carnegie Hall?" And, the answer: "Practice, practice, practice." A daily practice enables us to make course corrections and continue tracking towards our destination. Vision gives us our destination; daily practice helps us get there.

Daily practice can include meditation, strolling in nature, and any of the techniques I've introduced. I also use audio programs and journaling. Without a daily practice it's easy to succumb to what's known as "mission drift." Mission drift diverts you from living on purpose. Some detours take longer than others. Some ruin a life beyond repair.

3. Accountibality

There's no substitute for having someone to be accountable to. I'm a professional writer and I'm not lazy but, truth be told, I wouldn't produce much without my own coaches and deadlines. Deadlines are connected to checks. Coaches hold my feet to the fire.

You can be accountable to a parent, a spouse, a friend, a boss, a spiritual teacher, an employer, a coach, etc. Ultimately, you are accountable to yourself; that's who you really make your promises to.

4. Get Going

Ironically, success in life always comes down to taking action. But, how do we know what the right action is? And why would we keep acting when we don't want to (like, getting out of bed on dark, wet mornings to write or jog)? Many people make to-do lists and stay busy. That's old thinking, mental imposition, it's usually a struggle, and we procrastinate on the hard stuff. "Where there is no vision the to-do list perishes."

Motivation that lasts arises from the inside as a compelling vision that pulls us forward through daily actions to get the results we want.

We vision. We develop a daily practice to course correct and keep progressing towards our goals. We use an accountability buddy to help us keep the promises we've made with ourselves. We take vision-led action s every day and a very different future begins to develop.

Our personal lives begin to work and we contribute. And, as we age, we notice something approaching from the future:

When death comes
Like the hungry bear in autumn;
when death comes and takes all the bright
coins from his purse
to buy me, and snaps a purse shut;

When death comes
Like the measle–pox;
When death comes
Like an iceberg between the shoulder blades,
I want to step through the door full of
Curiosity wondering:
What is it going to be like, that cottage of darkness?

When it's over, I want to say: all my life
I was a bride married to amazement.
I was the bridegroom, taking the world into my arms.

When it's over, I don't want to wonder
if I have made of my life something
particular, and real.

I don't want to find myself sighing and frightened,
or full of argument.

I don't want to end up simply having visited this world.

~ Mary Oliver

death

Breath of compassion, five-pointed star
Breathe down on me from Your eternal sky
So I may radiate Your tender humility
And enter Your radiance when I die.

~ Sufi Prayer by Andrew Harvey

Death is a taboo subject in our culture. We prefer to distract ourselves with bright objects of every kind. So, in order to break through that denial and make this theme personal, I am devoting this chapter to a consideration of facing personal death.

Imagine boarding a plane with no landing gear, or discovering that fact in mid flight. This is exactly how we live. We know we're going to die. We know it because no one has avoided it yet, but we have no idea what it means. We try to not even think about it and we rarely prepare for it.

When someone close to us dies we may be overwhelmed by unfamiliar and uncomfortable emotions like grief and, not knowing how to deal with these strong emotions, we may go numb. Or, we may be jolted awake and start to wonder...

I spend three days with my aged mother in a Canadian hospice just before she dies. Whenever the effect of pain killing drugs abates, she speaks with regret. "Why did I work so hard? I should have had tea with the girls more often."

She dies in the dark, alone and confused. I drive home in the dark, pondering how insane we are to not prepare for the reality of death.

"Death and taxes" are the only two sure things, they say. Some people are clever enough to avoid paying taxes but none of us get out of here alive. In our culture, death is a problem of denial. Until we learn how to deal with this personally, we will remain blind to the potential death of our species. I call this The Titanic Problem.

the titanic problem

It didn't make any difference if a passenger had dessert or not on that fateful night when the great ship went down. A heated argument, a rejected offer, hopes and dreams — they all drowned with their owners. Every human drama played out on a sinking stage.

Here's an interesting question: If passengers knew they had just hours to live, how might that have changed their behavior?

If *we* discover that we have scant years to live, how might that change *our* behavior? Could that knowing elevate us above the pettiness of everyday squabbles? Could we begin to consider the meaning of both life and death, to discover values previously obscured by our fear and ignorance? Could we make significant changes in our lives, motivated by a healthy sense of urgency? Could we finish what we started?

Could facing death help us honor and actualize the "now or never" urgings of our soul and prepare us to take bold action relative to our global plight?

Stephen Jenkinson wrote in *Die Wise*: "It seems to take a monstrous turn of the Wheel, an unhinging of our plans, a big hole blown in our belief about how things should be for us to begin thinking about these things at all, let along deciding to live otherwise." [1]

Clue # 9:
What was found in the Great Pyramid
that now lives in cyber space?

We travel many miles to experience a winter storm hitting Long Beach on Vancouver Island. Luxuriating in a hot tub with my wife while the wind and rain rages outside, I am suddenly compelled to go to the ocean.

Unable to refuse this internal order, I dress and drive a brief distance, park, take off my shoes, and wade into the frigid waves. The rain is driving sideways so I'm quickly soaked to the bone. It's pitch dark, but for the lancing beam from a circling lighthouse beacon.

I brace myself knee deep in the waves, gusts, and rain, barely able to stand. Suddenly, the light illuminates a giant bird swooping past my head. My consciousness floods with an incredible awareness: I am given the day of my death. It's simultaneously shocking and reassuring. If this intuition proves accurate, I'll be here awhile longer.

Returning home the next day, I buy a countdown timer and set it for the big day (it actually says that on the clock, "The Big Day," with clip art fireworks). It sits on my desk now where I can watch the days, hours, minutes, and seconds of my life counting down. The message is clear: seize this moment, time is running out.

more from nature

A male chimp in Sweden has stirred excitement by storing a cache of stones to hurl at visitors," the BBC reports. "Santino, a chimpanzee in a zoo north of Stockholm, proves that animals can prepare for future events. These observations convincingly show that our fellow apes do consider the future in a very complex way," said scientist Mathias Osvath, reporting to the Associated Press.

Osvath began studying Santino after zoo staff found his stone supplies twelve years ago. What impressed Osvath most — beyond Santino's "highly developed consciousness" — was his tapping of water-weakened portions of concrete to pull out pieces of rock. Other studies have suggested consciousness in apes, but "now we have this spontaneous behavior, which is always in some sense better evidence," said Osvath." [2]

starting with what really matters

Clearly, other than birth, death is the single most important event for all of us. That we avoid thinking about our death confirms our most successful trait as humans: denial. So, bucking that trend, lean into your impending death and wonder: "How old will I be and where will I be when I die? What will it feel like? What kind of death do I want?"

When I first asked myself these questions, I imagined ...

> *I am back on Maui, where I met my wife and where we lived for seven years. I time travel to the last moments of my life to create a powerful famory. I feel peace, contentment with my life, gratitude for all the love I have received and given, and deep joy for my many friendships. I know that I am leaving the world with a few good seeds for a brighter future. I savor the satisfaction of arriving at this final moment feeling "well done."*

Now is the time to begin creating that final memory. Knowing how you want to feel when you die helps you make life choices to create that emotional result well before. Asking, "What kind of death do I want?" means that you begin taking care with how you live now, to build towards that final experience. The means determine the end.

None of us can know ahead of time how and when we will die. I don't believe that the death moment I divined is guaranteed to happen on schedule or the famory I created is a done deal. There are a million factors that could change this, none of which I have any control over. Will I actually make it back to Maui? Who knows?

But it really doesn't matter all that much. I am using my "target" to generate the feeling I want to experience in those last moments, whenever and wherever they turn out to be. Having created my famory, I'm experiencing that feeling right now. Vision first, results now.

Remember what you do when you travel? You prepare ahead of time. Shouldn't we do something similar with death? After all, we can't be sure we'll make it to Chicago. But we know we'll die. Shouldn't our preparations include both physical arrangements and imagining/ visioning how we would like to feel?

Deciding how you want to feel when you die and choosing to feel that way right now changes everything. You'll find that you begin to make choices based on what best enables you to sustain that feeling state. For instance, if you want to feel peace when you die, you might find yourself choosing to attend a group meditation rather than going to the bar to watch football. Another time, it might be the opposite. The friendship you share watching a game with buddies might be a warm memory on that big day.

My mother died with regret, mourning her unconscious priorities. That's not unusual. Imagine if she had visited her death in imagination long before it arrived. She could have decided then how she wanted to feel and made different choices. That would have prepared her for a profoundly different final few days. Actually, it would have changed her life.

Imagine if she had embraced a feeling intention to relax, to be happy, to hang out more and not do so much work. What if she had chosen to spend more quality time with her children and grandchildren? What if she had lived with the feeling that would give her, every day? She could have done whatever it took to sustain and increase that feeling and ride it all the way to the end.

let's finish what we started

How do you want to feel in that moment just before you breathe your last breath? Will you feel regret like my mother felt — like so many people feel as they reflect on a life of missed opportunities — or the fulfillment of a life well lived? How about feeling satisfaction, pride, peace and contentment, deep gratitude? Identify your priority qualities now, choose them, and start feeling that way.

As Commander Jean Luc Picard commanded
on *Star Trek, The Next Generation*:

"Make it so."

ಞ

Does showing up to be with someone in deep struggle
sound like a weakness? Is accepting accountability weak?
Is stepping up to the plate after striking out
a sign of weakness?

No. Vulnerability sounds like truth and feels like courage.
Truth and courage aren't always comfortable, but they're never
weakness.

~ Brené Brown

vision

Mother
Pillar of Fire
In this darkening desert
Help me follow you
Across the burning sands
Of my hopelessness and despair
To the country where your splendor reigns
And all the rocks and rivers chant your name.

~ Romanus Melodus

Clue # 10:
What used to be visible that has become invisible?

Indigenous cultures tend to be much more in touch with the reality of death than we are. They talk about living with death on the shoulder and may say, "It's a good day to die."

Death is a taboo subject in our culture, so we are ill prepared to deal with everything that accompanies this phenomenon all of us will experience.

It's possible to develop a vision for anything, including one's death. In fact, that's the next practice, described at the end of this chapter. This may seem like a morbid idea. It's not. Becoming comfortable with the event, knowing it's coming and preparing for it with a detailed famory of what you want those last moments to be like is akin to divining the name of a dragon. It's how you get power over something.

Poet extraordinaire Mary Oliver, who wrote the death poem we just featured, offers an inspiring vision of self worth in this poem, *Wild Geese*.

> *You do not have to be good.*
> *You do not have to walk on your knees*
> *For one hundred miles through the desert,*
> *repenting.*
> *You only have to let the soft animal of your*
> *body love what it loves.*
>
> *Tell me about despair, yours, and I will tell*
> *you mine.*
> *Meanwhile the world goes on.*
> *Meanwhile the sun and the clear pebbles of*
> *rain*
> *Are moving across the landscapes,*
> *Over the prairies and the deep trees,*
> *Mountains and rivers.*
>
> *Meanwhile the wild geese, high in the clean*
> *blue air,*
> *Are heading home again.*
> *Whoever you are, no matter how lonely,*
> *The world offers itself to your imagination,*
> *Calls to you like the wild geese, harsh and*
> *exciting—*
> *Over and over announcing your place*
> *In the family of things.* [1]

Coming home to "nature as ourselves" is a path of no return, happily, because it returns us to the one whole world where we belong. Whoever first said, "Once you have seen the city, it's hard to go back to the farm" predicted the modern malady of alienation from nature.

Here in the twenty-first century our very continuance as a species now compels us to reconfigure that saying: "Once we've reconnected with nature, it's impossible to go back to urban isolation."

And, once we've *truly* connected with nature we have also reconnected with the Divine, for the Divine lives in everything, in "the family of things."

We can fulfill this dream right now without a forest or a yoga mat. Just tune in. Tune in and get ready to close your eyes for a brief moment of visionary connection. First, read the short paragraph on the following page:

Close your eyes, tune in, and feel.
Notice: There is blood rushing through your veins.
Your nervous system is busy, brain synapses are firing,
thoughts are winging,
feelings are surging and ebbing.
Explore your senses: Listen. Smell. Taste. Touch. Feel.
Take another moment, then open your eyes and truly see.

Take a moment to close your eyes and explore your senses like this, then return to the text.

Opening your eyes now, look for a plant in your room. If there's none, get up and go to a window to catch a glimpse of nature. Tune in to one being amongst the many living forms in your visual field and give it your full attention. Pause to do this and notice what you feel as you do.

Welcome back. How did you feel? *What* did you feel? Nothing? Something? Every relationship requires attention. In this case, you're experimenting with a new kind of relationship, new for most of us. You and nature don't speak the same language yet but you can and will, *if* you invest in the relationship.

When we think different, we see different. When you develop the habit of including nature, wherever you are, you begin to think differently – again, this is something you have to experience for yourself – so you see differently. Your vision transforms and you begin to truly see ... that something wonderful is happening in every moment.

Life is flourishing!

another nature sampler

Light provides plants with energy, a system for telling time and an impetus to grow big enough to escape the confines of shade. Plant biologist Joanne Chory recently identified the exact protein that triggers stems and stalks to grow taller. The protein, called PIF7, senses the arrangement of light around the plant — and if the plant is in shade, will spur the entire plant to grow taller and seek sun." [2]

That plant has a relationship with the sun. Do you have a relationship with a plant in your room or one you can see out the window?

We have walled ourselves away from our best friends, hiding inside our mansions and hovels and skyscrapers and stadiums and even riding rockets into space, while becoming increasingly alienated from our planetary home and all the species we share it with.

The images of mountains and waterfalls we use as screen savers are a poor substitute for the multi-dimensional experience of our home nest. Remember when the world was flat? It's flat again — on a screen. But nature is not flat, it's not a backdrop for life, it *is* life. Our visits to the natural world are not supposed to be temporary distractions from more important busyness.

coming home

The return of the prodigal son is both a Biblical story and the name of the last painting from Dutch master Rembrandt, known for the introspective themes he wove into his great works. The painting depicts a young man on his knees, head buried in his father's breast.

This story is fleshed out in the Gospel of Luke. A man's younger son "gathered all he had and took a journey into a far country, and there he squandered his property in reckless living. And when he had spent everything, a severe famine arose in that country..." [3] This describes where we are right now. Humans *are* that younger son, a careless teenager on the planet. And, what are the results of our immature actions? "A severe famine." That's one under-stated way to describe it.

The story continues: "... when he came to himself, he said, "I will arise and go to my father, and I will say to him, 'Father, I have sinned against heaven and before you. I am no longer worthy to be called your son. Treat me as one of your hired servants.'"

Having awakened to our own irresponsible behavior, how we've wasted our own fortune and plundered the earth, can we embody the son's honestly and humility? Can we admit to the damage our leaving and recklessness have caused and feel the same remorse?

Here's what happened in this story when the son returned: "... while he was still a long way off, his father saw him and felt compassion, and ran and embraced him and kissed him. And the son said to him, 'Father, I have sinned against heaven and before you. I am no longer worthy to be called your son.' But the father said to his servants, 'Bring quickly the best robe, and put it on him, and put a ring on his hand, and shoes on his feet. And bring the fattened calf and kill it, and let us eat and celebrate. For this my son was dead, and is alive again; he was lost, and is found.' And they began to celebrate."

The son confessed to himself, then to his father. Humility, remorse, forgiveness. "He was lost, and is found." That was the father's attitude, not, "Where have you been, how could you have been so foolish?"

Nature welcomes us home without judgment. So does the Divine. (contrary to how God shows up in the Old Testament). That welcome is waiting for us now, the same welcome I experience here in our Oregon forest. The Divine lives in every stream, in every tree and breeze. We can return to this world and find that we are welcomed home.

There's a poignant moment at the end of the film, *The Bridge on the River Kwai*, when Alex Guinness's character stands, takes off his hat, and says something like, "What have I done?" He realizes that he has been blinded by arrogant pride. All of us could have our own moment like that. Except, or course, we'd rather not die in a hail of bullets!

How lost have we been, wandering in civilization's counterfeit world, squandering our inheritance of primal belonging. But remember what happened after the son came to his senses and turned back towards home: "... while he was still a long way off, his father saw him and felt compassion, and ran and embraced him and kissed him." Surely it's time that we return home to Mother Nature and to Father Spirit.

Do you identify with the son or the father in this story? If we've been the wayward son, let's come home so we can be the father for others, seeing through those blessing eyes with forgiveness and no-strings-attached welcome. That's true vision!

Practice Five - Vision

"I say it, see it, and feel it."

In this practice you will create two visions, one for your life and one for your death. The purpose is to develop a compass for navigating your life.

Your spell is "I say it, I see it, I feel it," a reminder of our visioning process. The movement is a flinging forward motion followed by an immediate attraction, a sense of being pulled by your vision.

The core feeling is confidence and you create two images, one for your life and one for your death.

The practice has two parts. First, conjure up an image for your life. When I did this, years ago, I came up with a rocket ship on the launch pad. Initially, nothing much was going on. Over time, as I checked back on this image, activity increased, then the rocket blasted off. Now, it's nearing free fall.

In other words, your image is alive.

The image for your death is very different; it's actually a famory. Intuit when you may die and travel forward to that moment. Follow the "say it, see, it, feel it" formula to create the detailed famory, as real as possible.

Visit the scene of your death regularly. Notice that, over time, it becomes a welcomed experience, rather than something to dread. You are making friends with your death. It is becoming a compelling vision to pull you forward in your life.

༊

stand

You must stand for something!

It does not have to be grand,
but it must be a positive that brings light
to someone else's darkness.

~ Anthony Carmona

Clue # 11:
What requires our agreement
to enable it to influence our lives?

"They," whoever they are, say that if you don't stand for something, you'll fall for anything. What do *you* stand for?

A handful of courageous activists like Mahatma Gandhi, Rosa Parks, Martin Luther King, Mother Theresa, Gloria Steinem, and Nelson Mandela, have changed the world because of their stand. But the idea of taking a stand, being selfless, living values-first, has become the perceived exception rather than the widely adopted norm.

If it's true that only a few individuals actually stand for something and persevere to help bring about constructive change in society, what are the rest of us here for? To make *their* lives more difficult? To slow down the process of positive change? Or, might we join them and do our share?

It's been said that if you aren't part of the solution you're part of the problem. No one likes to think of themselves as a problem but how many of us are standing for nothing in particular right now except our own existence and whatever immediate pleasures we can get? This describes our narcissistic culture.

Ask yourself where you stand. Consult your heart: are you living fully in your deep passion right now? And, what exactly *do* you stand for?

The two may seem mutually exclusive — taking a stand and living with passion – but those well-known activists I just mentioned were always passionate about what they stood for. It was never just an intellectual exercise or a duty, not if it had an impact.

Remember the movie *Network*? Now, there was someone taking a passionate stand. If you remember, Peter Finch's character exhorted viewers of his radical television news show to go to their windows, open them, and shout: "I'm mad as hell and I'm not going to take this anymore!" Thousands in his audience did exactly that in the movie. As we watched at the theater and in our homes many of us got enrolled in the outrage. I know that some viewers even got up and shouted from their own windows.

But, in the end, what happened out here in the real world? What action did any of us take relative to the themes of the film, which included economic monopolization enabled by an increasingly disempowering mainstream media?

Since that film aired in 1976 those aspects of our society have deteriorated much further into a quagmire of feudal dysfunction, with little resistance from most of us. Why did so few of us do anything to stop mass media becoming a tool for propagandists to enslave the masses? What about hate radio? We may wring our hands today about Rush Limbaugh and Alex Jones but this phenomenon developed way back in the thirties. Read *Radio Priest: Charles Coughlin, The Father of Hate Radio,* by Donald Warren.

Seeing something inspiring in a movie, reading it online or in a book, we may get informed and even gain an expanded understanding, but all too often that results only in a few moments of emotion and then ... we're done. What has changed in us? Nothing. Let's watch another show.

An obvious recent example in America was the campaign and election of President Obama. "Hope and change" was his theme and millions rallied around it, thrilled with new possibilities. Eight disappointing years later, we've seen just how difficult it is to change the status quo in Washington.

"Hope and change" was a great campaign slogan, it won an election. What's happened to our hope? How much real change happened? To say it's been disappointing is a gross understatement. Who knows why these dreams failed? Many would argue that the President himself hasn't much actual power. An obstructionist Congress didn't help.

Regardless, instead of blaming others, what about you? What do you stand for? Do you have vision, a daily practice, someone to be accountable to, and will you take one action after another to turn your life in the direction you want and give your gifts in the world?

Those of us who live this kind of life *can* become discouraged. A friend told me about a letter he received from a veteran environmentalist, someone he considered one of the strongest people he knew. She had been working on tragic issues in Africa, helping an indigenous village confront cruelty and oppression. After years of this noble work she gave up.

Her letter began, "By the time you read this I will be dead." Her heart was broken and so was her spirit. She just couldn't take any more. She chose to end her life rather than continuing to confront madness and cruelty. So, let's learn a hard lesson from this tragic story.

Never forget that we need each other.

Never forget to ask for help when we need it.

And ... we always need it.

nature break

It seems that plants can recognize kin, says Brandon Keim of *Wired* Magazine. In a paper published in the November *American Journal of Botany*, (biologist Susan) Dudley describes how *Impatiens pallida*, a common flowering plant, "devotes less energy than usual to growing roots when surrounded by relatives. In the presence of genetically unrelated *Impatiens*, individuals grow their roots as fast as they can. Apparently plants recognize their relatives via chemicals exuded from their roots, and choose to share available nutrients with them." [1]

Taking a stand includes acknowledging that we all have our personal shadows. It's incomplete to work in the world without working within ourselves.

'The shadow," wrote Carl Jung (in 1963), is "that hidden, repressed, for the most part inferior and guilt-laden personality whose ultimate ramifications reach back into the realm of our animal ancestors and so comprise the whole historical aspect of the unconscious." [2]

You cannot see your own shadow. You *can* acknowledge that you have one / many, and you *can* invite others to help you see what you cannot see for yourself. Unless you do, what is suppressed within you will erupt under the pressure of circumstances.

This reminds us of the being/doing relationship. There is more involved, especially for quantum activists, than just doing noble things. Neither is it enough to heed inspiring words like these from John F. Kennedy: "Each time a person stands up for an ideal, or acts to improve the lot of others, or strikes out against injustice, he or she sends forth a tiny ripple of hope. And crossing each other from a million different centers of energy and daring, those ripples build a current that can sweep down the mightiest walls of oppression and resistance." [3]

Has that worked? Yes, we've made progress. But we haven't averted the threat of human near-term extinction. Without dismissing the value of Kennedy's stirring message, clearly something more is needed. We're exploring a radical alternative: the *way* we are broadcasts through all we do. This makes it imperative that we clean up our act.

facing our shadow

Modern mystic Andrew Harvey writes, "In authentic shadow work you will be compelled to discover that everything you hate in others lives in you – that everything you fear in the destructive forces raging in our world has a home in you in some dark corner, in an unacknowledged, unhealed fear or trauma, a hunger to be unique and special, or an unexamined desire for revenge." [4]

The stand we take begins within ourselves, refusing to demonize the forces "out there" by acknowledging that they also thrive in us. How do we break free of all this? The Prayer of St. Francis offers a profound perspective on what it means to face our shadows and take a stand.

> *Lord, make me an instrument of thy peace.*
> *Where there is hatred, let me sow love;*
> *Where there is injury, pardon;*
> *Where there is doubt, faith;*
> *Where there is despair, hope;*
> *Where there is darkness, light;*
> *Where there is sadness, joy.*
>
> *Oh Divine Master, grant that I may not so much seek*
> *To be consoled as to console,*
> *To be understood as to understand,*
> *To be loved as to love:*
> *For it is in giving that we receive,*
> *It is in pardoning that we are pardoned,*
> *It is in dying that we are born to eternal life.*

There can be great solace in prayer, and taking a stand for something you believe in *is* profoundly self-affirming. But it's not enough just to meditate. That is not an action in the world on its own.

Likewise, it's not enough to just march in the streets. Working on both the inner and the outer, we weave together the sacred with the pragmatic.

This defines the work of a quantum activist. We first take a stand inside ourselves, then we act, and the power of our inner commitment transmits our passion through everything we do. This is what can change the world.

Remember Bucky's trim tab?

If we are to survive as a species and thrive into the future we need trim-tab leadership. Will you become part of the trim tab and help lead the way?

అ

Security is mostly a superstition.
It does not exist in nature,
nor do the children of men as a whole experience it.
Avoiding danger is no safer in the long run than outright exposure.

Life is either a daring adventure, or nothing.

~ Helen Keller

multitudes

If someone with multiple personalities
threatens to kill himself,
is it considered a hostage situation?

~ George Carlin

Joanna Macy writes, "Because the relationship between self and world is reciprocal, it is not a question of first getting enlightened and then acting. As we work to heal the Earth, the Earth heals us; there is no need to wait. When we care enough to take risks we loosen the grip of the ego and begin to come home to our true nature. For, in the co–arising nature of things, the world itself, if we are bold to love it, acts through us." [1]

Can you be bold to love the world? Can you put your love for the world first? When you do, when it's the real thing, you discover that "you" is not really "I," it is "we." Such a fundamental identity shift is disruptive and liberating.

Clue # 12:
What moves faster than a speeding bullet
but is not Superman?

BTW, the clues scattered through PART TWO are disruptive by design. Before reprogramming can happen, de-programming must occur. Breakdown and then breakthrough, as the saying goes.

One way to coax ourselves towards this identity shift is to challenge the irrational but almost universal belief that we are the only truly intelligent species on the planet. Can a plant be *intelligent?* Some plant scientists insist plants *are* intelligent, since they can sense, learn, remember, and even react in ways that would be familiar to humans.

Michael Pollan, author of such books as *The Omnivore's Dilemma* and *The Botany of Desire*, wrote a New Yorker piece about developments in plant science.

> For the longest time, even mentioning the idea that plants could be intelligent was a quick way to being labeled a 'whacko', but no more, which might be comforting to people who have long talked to their plants or played music for them. The new research is in a field called plant neurobiology — which is something of a misnomer, because even scientists in the field don't agree that plants have neurons or brains. They have analogous structures. They have ways of taking all the sensory data they gather in their everyday lives, integrate it, and then behave in an appropriate way in response. And they do this without brains, which, in a way, is what's incredible about it, because we automatically assume you need a brain to process information. [2]

we contain multitudes

Interestingly, we may have been measuring intelligence in an unintelligent way! And perhaps our search for alien life forms should start closer to home? We are *not* alone as the only conscious species on this planet; we have *never* been alone, and we can *never* be anything but destructive as a single, separate "I" in sole possession of intelligence.

Individuation, the psychological norm for "growing up" – programming human isolation and domination over every other species — turns out to be a passport to insanity. We are not meant to exist in narcissistic bubbles as separate individuals. We live in a community of many, within and without. Walt Whitman wrote, "I am large. I contain multitudes."

Aspects of these multitudes show up as "selves," for instance in the array of roles we play from day to day, but most of us get stuck on just a few of them, or just one, the one we may come to believe is who we are. Then, without warning, some crazy self pops out like a cuckoo, embarrassing everyone. We all have a few of those characters in our cast. A little too much wine and out he or she explodes.

Our inability to control the many and reconcile ourselves to a multi-faceted identity is connected to our quest for the "one."

Who do we worship in the western world? What is the nature of our God? One old man. He has no wife and no family but for us, His eternal children who never grow up, apparently. *He* is our God, our one and only God. How many millions of people believe that fervently?

Today, here in the twenty-first century, when we can transplant hearts and send people into space, it's still heretical to dare suggest there's a feminine aspect to divinity. What's more, the truly faithful maintain that their particular angry male God is the only one and all others are abominations? Some believe it with enough white-hot passion to kill those who disagree.

Indigenous cultures knew God, not as a singular, separate being, but as spirits that animated every form. They did not worship a belief; their Spirit lived in nature and permeated all living things. There was no life without the Great Spirit. The white man's preference for concepts and harsh rules seemed crazy to them, and still does. How many millions have been killed in religious conflicts, pitting the champions of one single, conceptual being against another? Madness.

So, our identity problem has two paradoxical faces: a personal identity limited to the singular (when, in fact, we all contain multitudes), and a Divine being limited to the singular (when the Great Spirit lives in all and everything).

There's a further error. Howard Clinebell wrote about this in *Eco Therapy – Healing Ourselves, Healing the Earth*:

> To all these interdependent alienations must now be added the two-fold alienation from nature – from our own inner 'wildness' and from organic bonding with nature. This alienation is a bottom–line cause of violent behavior toward nature, toward our

bodies, and toward others perceived as 'wild.' Healing and preventing this violence involves healing the Earth alienation that is at their roots. Helping people learn to open themselves to be nurtured more deeply and often by nature is one crucial focus of holistic healing, teaching, and parenting. [3]

opening our hearts

We may justifiably fear the multitude we sense within us. Our complex and numerous emotions are ultimately uncontrollable, yet we are inhuman without them.

We can stuff our feelings, damning ourselves to a twilight limbo of robotic, armored existence, but sooner of later we *will* feel. This can produce outbursts of destructive, irrational behaviors – witness employee shootings that surprise everyone ("He was so quiet, polite, I would never have guessed...").

How many lonely individuals are out there feeling separate and alienated from others? As many as are disconnected from the Great Spirit that lives in everyone and everything and as many as have accepted a singular identity for themselves and denied their personal multitudes.

the real teacher

Walter R. Christie wrote in Howard Clinebell's book: "Nature is our teacher, because much of who we are is indistinguishable from her, although mystics who have gone before us say that in the higher realms of consciousness is revealed a world of pure light and energy that permeates all natural forms. However, we still have much to learn; we are gifted creatures, but we are dangerous creatures too." [4]

To survive and thrive requires feeling what we've feared to feel, to realize that we are only special in the same way that every other species is special. We are not singularly exceptional after all. We are uniquely ourselves, as is every other species. We are peers and we are connected.

I am, we are, a multitude.

⌒

21

imagery

*Imagery is the natural language of the emotions
and of the unconscious mind.
It also has a profound controlling influence on our nervous, endocrine,
and immune systems. Imagery should be thought of as a way of
working with the patient, rather than a way of treating
a particular disease or symptoms.*

~ from *An Overview of Interactive Guided Imagery* manual
by David Bresler, PhD and Martin Rossman, MD

I use interactive guided imagery in my mentoring practice and am deeply indebted to the work of David Bresler, PhD and Martin Rossman, MD for the work they have pioneered in their Academy for Guided Imagery. Key elements of what I offer clients is based in their breakthrough techniques, and this chapter includes many references to their wisdom.

I heartily recommend readers who are drawn to this kind of work to connect with the Academy through their web site: http://acadgi.com/ — Good guys, great work.

My coach guides me to the image of a turtle. The turtle represents how I sometimes act in social settings. A turtle can retreat inside his shell whenever he feels threatened and I am good at that. Coach Alan helps me develop another image — Curious George.

The next day I find myself at a half-day workshop on Implicit Bias. Suddenly I find myself connecting with people I would have previously ignored. Each person is a treasure chest that opens as I engage. Gone is my sense of superiority, my indifference, my judgments, my shyness. I am Curious George!

Clue # 13:
**What do we all have the same amount of
at birth and death?**

imagifi the future

Mad Max Fury Road, won six Oscars in 2015 in the categories of film editing, costume design, makeup and hairstyling, sound mixing and editing, and production design.

Do you notice anything unusual about that list? Every award relates to sights and sound, none to story. Films provide both, and if a picture is worth a thousand words, how many words are images worth, complete with sound? Millions, billions? This is how we *live* a story, through imagery, and this is how we create our personal future. These days we are also doing it collectively through the production and viewing of dystopian nightmare movies that millions of us watch.

Try to name movies that depict a happy future. If you Google "films about a positive future" you may find, as I did, one single movie: *2001, A Space Odyssey*, the 1968 masterpiece by Stanley Kubrick. Film reviewer Roger Ebert described it this way: "Alone among science fiction movies, '2001' is not concerned with thrilling us, but with inspiring our awe." [1]

Ebert attended the film premiere in Hollywood. Rock Hudson walked out. Some followed, others were restless. Hollywood slammed the film. It was too slow; it lacked the conflict necessary to make a good story.

Here's how Ebert described his experience of what Kubrick (in close collaboration with author Arthur C. Clarke) had created:

> *What he had actually done was make a philosophical statement about man's place in the universe, using images as those before him had used words, music, or prayer. And he made it in a way that invited us to contemplate it – not to experience it vicariously as entertainment, as we might in a good conventional science-fiction film – but to stand outside it as a philosopher might, and think about it.* [2]

Our portrayals of the future have changed dramatically over the 47 years, from *2001, A Space Odyssey* in 1968 to *Mad Max* in 2015, from a vision of future beauty and human transformation to a crazed wasteland.

Now, Google "films about a dystopian future." Wikepedia lists films from 1951 through 2015 and there are 182 of them. [3]

the power of guided imagery

We seem to be much more interested in and able to imagine a dark future than a bright one. Why is that? What's happened in those forty-seven years between *Odyssey* and *Mad Max*? Humanity seems to have decided that a nightmare is coming and we demand previews of coming distractions.

Films have become increasingly darker. Most of us don't make films but we do choose what we watch. No one is forcing us to fill ourselves with images of hell on the horizon. We can also use our own imagery to create what *we* want. Here's how:

Imagine a lemon. Picture it. Taste it. Be as detailed as possible. If you imagine it vividly, you will salivate. Notice that just reading the word "lemon" or thinking about it doesn't produce any saliva flow. Using imagery does. If imagining a lemon causes you to salivate, what happens when you are immersed in an image-rich film that casts future humans as hopeless, helpless victims? What effect might this have on us?

We don't salivate; we tremble.

Films like this tell us to be afraid and give up. Just keep on eating popcorn, there's nothing we can do but drink another coke and eat more chocolate.

Images stimulate specific neural and biochemical signals connected with escapism, defeat, and resignation. Using this same principle, we can use our imaginations to evoke positive imagery instead — like Kubrick did on the big screen — to envision a positive future for ourselves and a positive outcome for humanity.

Here's a stunning bit of fact from the teaching manual Bresler and Rossman developed. Using imagery is not a frivolous novelty; there's a considerable amount of brain science to validate its effectiveness.

When researchers have used a sophisticated technique called positron emission tomography [PET] to monitor the brain during imagery exercises, they found that the same parts of the cerebral cortex are activated whether people imagine something or actually experience it. This suggests that picturing visual images activates the optic cortex, and imagining that you are listening to music arouses the auditory cortex, and conjuring up tactile sensations stimulates the sensory cortex.

Plus, vivid imagery can send a message from the cerebral cortex to the lower brain centers, including the limbic system, the emotional center of the brain. From there, the message is relayed to the endocrine system and the autonomic nervous system, which can affect a range of bodily functions, including heart rate, perspiration, and blood pressure. Many clinicians believe that the more fully you imagine something, the more 'real' it seems to the brain and the greater the amount of information sent to the nervous system. This is one reason it's helpful to use as many senses as possible during guided imagery sessions. [4]

I use imagery unconsciously all day long and so do you. The question is, *how* do we use it? Imagery affects our physiology. Think sex. Bresler and Rossman added: "Responsible for everything from physical attraction to orgasm intensity, the brain is undoubtedly your most important sexual organ." [5]

Imagery is the language of the unconscious mind; it doesn't use words. That means that to try only using words to change your experience – for instance by reciting affirmations like "I am rich!" – is futile. Gary Larson depicted this in a 1983 cartoon: A man is talking to his dog. He says "I've had it. You stay out of the garbage! Understand, Ginger? Stay out of the garbage or else!" The next panel is entitled, What Dogs Hear. "Blah blah Ginger, blah blah blah blah blah Ginger blah blah."

We need more than words to communicate with our subconscious, which is where the patterns and programs that govern our creativity reside. Using interactive guided imagery techniques enable us to open a dialogue with our unconscious. This can reveal deep secrets relating to our health, career, and relationships (particularly the relationship with ourselves).

Guided imagery can change moods. Crafting future fantasies can help us shift worry and fear to calmness and courage. Over time, this builds self-esteem and confidence because we are changing our actual experience.

Through guided imagery work a person develops an inner support system to combat their inner critic, which barks at all of us all day, every day. "You failed before, here you go again. Why did you do that? That was stupid. See him looking at you; he hated what you just said." All of us have an inner critic, but we can also have an inner supporter. In fact, we can have a team of supporters, if we create them.

For starters, I help clients connect with one inner advisor who begins to provide the guidance, encouragement, and enthusiastic support that a spouse, friends, and family are unable or unwilling to provide, for whatever reason. Clients learn to employ imagery to overcome old, negative habits and create new, positive ones. Using imagery to represent both the critics and the helpers establishes constructive habits, for instance, learning how to generate a feeling of inner calm in the midst of turmoil.

Using imagery can also help us turn insights into action. Nothing gets done without taking action. But we won't take action, at least not consistently and especially when we don't want to, and we won't know what actions to take, unless we've developed that compelling vision of a rewarding future. An image can serve to anchor that vision. For instance, you might anchor your vision for a revitalized marriage to the image of two swans swimming together gracefully. Swans mate for life so there's a great subliminal message in this image.

five imagery techniques

We can learn to use imagery as a normal part of aware living.

Imagery literacy develops the imagination, strengthens and clarifies navigation skills in the Wonder Field, and enables us to think new and act differently. Imagery experts use scores of techniques. Here are five that introduce the basics.

1. **Finding your safe place:** The first and simplest technique is to create an imaginary place where you feel safe. Imagine a familiar location in nature such as a beach, a forest with a stream, a meadow in the woods, or make up a utopian vision.

2. **Meeting your inner advisor:** Once present in this safe space, you can invite a guide to appear. This can be a person, an animal, or some aspect of nature like a giant oak tree or a deep, powerful river. The advisor needs to know you, to love you, to have some wisdom to share, and to want to get actively engaged in your life.

3. **Dialoguing with the advisor(s):** Anyone can develop a team of advisors over time, but we start with one and initiate a dialogue in order to gain helpful, practical insights. Most people are surprised how easy it is to ask a question of the advisor and get an immediate and sometimes surprising reply.

4. **Creating specific images:** When a client tells me what they want to work on I often ask what image might represent their issue. They can then talk with that image directly to find out what it needs or what message it has. Another approach is to create an image that represents what their life is like right now and another one for what they would like their future to be.

5. **Being a community**: Life changes when we welcome our guides and images as a normal part of who we are. Suddenly, we're not alone; we have help to understand what's really going on in a crisis and we are able to ask for guidance for important decisions.

imagination becomes perception

Remember when you learned to drive a car? It was so difficult to focus on everything all at once. There was the steering, the looking in the rear view mirror, the gas pedal, the brake, the turn signals, etc. Gradually, it all became familiar and then automatic, until you were able to just enjoy driving. That's called unconscious competency.

Developing and perfecting imagery skills happens the same way and regular practice is the path to mastery. I often say to clients: "Those who practice every day gets results, those who don't, don't."

"Constant instant practice" is a term I learned from Dr.'s Bresler and Rossman. They describe this as "allowing a frequent occurrence in daily life (such as a telephone ringing) to become a reminder to practice." [6] For example, you might be working on your marriage relationship and may have determined that you want to experience more deep love and trust with your partner. So, you might anchor in the ringing phone to that feeling. The phone rings, you see his or her number displayed, and this triggers a feeling of deep love.

There's a turning point in working with imagery. At first, it's just imagination. But at some point a person realizes that it's also perception. You're not *just* imagining that feeling of deep love with your partner, you're also perceiving it. You're not *just* imagining a guide, you're perceiving her — this aspect of yourself — and her wisdom is your own inner knowing. You're not *just* imagining a future outcome, you're actually having the experience.

Past, present, and future coexist in the quantum field of deep time. You taste that lemon in your imagination and you salivate. The phone rings and you feel love for your partner.

The Slinky Effect activates: the physical chases the imaginal to grow the future you have envisioned into brick and mortar reality. A quantum activist is at work.

more surprises from nature

Michael Pollan writes:

> How plants sense and react is still somewhat unknown. They don't have nerve cells like humans, but they do have a system for sending electrical signals and even produce neurotransmitters, like dopamine, serotonin, and other chemicals the human brain uses to send signals. We don't know why they have them, whether this was just conserved through evolution or if it performs some sort of information processing function. We don't know. There's a lot we don't know.

And chalk up another human-like ability — memory. Pollan describes an experiment done by animal biologist Monica Gagliano. She presented research that suggests the mimosa pudica plant can learn from experience. Pollan states, "merely suggesting a plant could learn was so controversial that her paper was rejected by ten scientific journals before it was finally published.

Mimosa is a plant, which looks something like a fern, that collapses its leaves temporarily when it is disturbed. So Gagliano set up a contraption that would drop the mimosa plant, without hurting it. When the plant dropped, as expected, its leaves collapsed. She kept dropping the plants every five to six seconds. After five or six drops, the plants would stop responding, as if they'd learned to tune out the stimulus as irrelevant. This is a very important part of learning — to learn what you can safely ignore in your environment.[7]

thank you Mr. Kubrick

We are a species under threat and our storytelling proves it.

As observed a few pages ago, there are a plethora of films that employ vivid imagery to depict a nightmare future (182 listed online), and a dearth of films presenting anything uplifting (just 1 listed). *2001: A Space Odyssey* is the only inspiring film I could find mentioned online and I'd like to close this chapter and PART TWO with a final quote from reviewer Roger Ebert about this remarkable film which presents a possible future that includes positive human transformation:

> Only a few films are transcendent, and work upon our minds and imaginations like music or prayer ... (This film) says to us: We became men when we learned to think. Our minds have given us the tools to understand where we live and who we are. Now it is time to move on to the next step, to know that we live not on a planet but among the stars, and that we are not flesh but intelligence. [8]

> *We are both intelligence and flesh.*
> *We live in the planet; we belong here.*
>
> *Simultaneously, we are at home amongst*
> *the stars. Our imagination can weave these*
> *together into the transformation*
> *we are envisioning,*
> *from separation to oneness.*

All of a sudden we become aware that,
instead of our being born into the world,
this world has simply been born in us.

Wherever we look we are seeing
not what we depend on for our survival
but what now depends on us
in order to survive.

For through our divine awareness
we are the source
and creator and maintainer of the universe
just as a tree sustains its branches and shoots.

...Everything is inside you now, rooted deep into your being.

And with the entire universe inside of you,
where in reality it always has been,
you can sense for the first time how much power you hold
in the palm of your hand."

For the whole world
– whatever you experience or perceive –
is just buds on the tree that you are."

~ Peter Kingsley

⮑

Why are we so desperate to escape the material world?

Is it really so bleak?
Or could it be, rather, that we have made it bleak:
obscured its vibrant mystery
with our ideological blinders, severed its infinite connectedness with our
categories, suppressed its spontaneous order
with our pavement, reduced its infinite variety
with our commodities,
shattered its eternity with our time-keeping,
and denied its abundance with our money system?

If so, then we are misguided if we appeal
to a non-material spiritual realm
for salvation from the prison of materiality."

– Thomas Berry

three - engage

Creating something out of nothing is stressful
and requires a lot of 'work.'
Revealing something that is already there
requires considerably less effort
because it already exists.

It's more like excavating than building.
That is what we mean by effortlessness.

The reason Michelangelo was able to see David
already in the stone is that David was inside him.

~ Dr. Christine Ranck and Christopher Lee Nutter

navigation

Once you are touched by a living intelligence
from out there, you are changed.
It is nearly impossible not to be.

The living reality of that experience works on the self,
undermining the old paradigm,
and you begin to, more and more frequently,
step outside the normal habituated boundaries
of the Western world.

You begin to enter an older, wilder,
less domesticated world, the place barbarians inhabit,
where the hair begins to grow long,
where wild lights begin to gleam in the eye.

You begin to enter the wilderness that still lies underneath
the concrete of the civilized world.

... Through the lives of those whose boundaries have thinned,
we catch glimpses of the shimmer of infinity
in the face of the other,
catch glimpses through the doors of perception
of the metaphysical background of the world.

~ Stephen Harrod Buhner

Way back in the Introduction, I referenced what I called "Timothy Leary's mistake" when he said: "Tune in, turn on, drop out." I speculated about what society might have become had he advised: "Tune in, turn on, engage."

Engagement is what we explore throughout PART THREE in seven chapters. This first chapter gives you a preview of coming attractions and introduces the concept of following your heartbreak to discover your destined contribution.

Chapter twenty-three presents the solution to clues you followed throughout PART TWO and introduces my own 2025 initiative in detail.

Chapter twenty-four outlines what a B.H.A.G. is (Big Hairy Audacious Goal) and offers ideas for creating your own.

Chapter twenty-five introduces "discovery" as a practice and provides details about The New World Party on May 1, 2025.

Chapter twenty-six considers transmission — how we impact the Wonder Field — otherwise known in our context as entrainment, and re-emphasizes the importance of asking (and answering) "Who can one person be?"

Chapter twenty-seven reframes the activities of your life as a garden that needs constant, intelligent tending.

The final chapter zeroes in on your quantum activist assignment for 2025, with examples to inspire you. We learn about the network that is developing and complete with an inspiring practice that brings everything in this book together in one ten-minute process.

a primary realization

Early on, I mentioned a primary realization and have been hinting at it throughout these pages. It's time for the full reveal so you can have this installed as the core processor of your new operating system as we progress our learning adventure into strategies about "what to do."

This revelation could turn out to be as anti-climactic or profound as telling a fish about water. We live in this realization without knowing it — it's that natural. But it often eludes both our industrious seeking and our clever inventiveness. For good reason.

Once glimpsed, honestly contemplated, realized, and embodied, life is never the same again.

In searching for the ideal words to deliver this insight, I've chosen to access the crazy wisdom of Peter Kingsley again, this time from his epic volume, *Reality*, because he puts it so clearly and concisely.

> "... *when we live the illusion to the full, to its furthest limits,*
> *we are nothing but reality fulfilling its own longing.*
> *In spite of the appearances,*
> *regardless of all our seeming limitations,*
> *we are simply reality completing itself.*" [1]

You are "reality completing itself." And, you are instructed to "live the illusion to the full." This means being "generative," creating as a fully engaged participant. I wonder how many of us have hung back, hesitating to commit ourselves whole-heartedly because we didn't embody this principle? Uh, almost all of us.

Did we fear that full commitment would legitimize and empower conditions we judged unworthy of our attention? Did we feel it was futile, unsafe, not worth the effort, or that something better was coming after we died? When we dropped out, just what did we imagine was left?

Could a fish "drop out" from water?

implications

This solves your primary challenge in being here. Once you've embraced yourself as "reality completing itself," there is no choice but to greet every moment with appreciation. Here is the raw material offered to complete yourself (and reality). And it's how we can effectively navigate our lives.

Nothing and no one can be turned away when you fully engage in this way. Our attention comes to attention, fully attending the details of now, as if there is no other moment ... because now we know there isn't.

Deep time is the term I've used for this, while Buhner referred to it as "the metaphysical background of the world." We develop our mastery for traveling in deep time right here, right now, in the only place and time that *is* real.

The clock stops and so does our life in prison. Freedom, it turns out, has always been an inside job.

You may look up and glance around the room, wherever it is you are reading. It probably looks deceptively similar to how it looked before you began reading this chapter. It's similar but not the same. You've crossed a threshold, you've entered the wilderness, you've engaged.

The comedian Stephen Wright tells a joke about waking up one morning to discover that everything in his apartment has been stolen and replaced with an exact duplicate. He tells his neighbor what has happened and she asks, "Who are you?"

You are a quantum activist, present in service to reality and yourself and eager to help relieve the suffering of others: by completing yourself in every situation, and sticking around for as long as it takes.

Imagine the implications of full engagement. It means embracing illusion *as reality* and ourselves as *reality completing itself,* and not being in a hurry to get out of here. This realization propels you and me to a moment of decision: to live full on, with *nothing* held back, or not.

And when would we make that decision? Now ... or never.

entering the wilderness together

To be "in this world but not of it" is the ultimate challenge. It's so much easier to withdraw from the craziness or get lost in it. Trauma specialists identify isolated incidents of extreme stress but who considers the daily damage from living in this madhouse prison called civilization? Especially when we are simultaneously the inmates and the wardens? Especially, when we realize it and don't have support to walk through the door that's just swung open, unsure of what lies beyond.

As Buhner wrote in the opening quote, "You begin to enter an older, wilder, less domesticated world." Actually, it's safe here and there are many others. The enlightenment we've struggled to find, retreating into solitary confinement rushes towards us when we engage together.

Regardless of widely believed religious pronouncements, the material world is *not* an inferior world. To agree with that judgment would be to accuse the Creator of making a grand mistake. If we add in the concept of original sin and believe that the same God made us vulnerable to temptation, then not only does He do shoddy work but He needs therapy. Perhaps we've just made Him in our own image.

What a crazy belief: give us delicious bait – this material world complete with all its delights and sorrows – and dare us to take a bite.

No, this world, this unfinished symphony we dance around in every day, is a wonderful world — except for the horror we have manufactured, often fueled by faith in beliefs of one kind or another. Every word in this book invites you to place your faith elsewhere, in the unfolding reality of now and your ability to make a difference through unreserved engagement.

Why have you undertaken this journey of personal transformation?

Because you've come to understand that "now or never" describes this crisis moment of the twenty-first century. Because you agree that human survival is no longer possible or required, that human transformation is our only hope. Because you get the urgent truth that either I / you / we come together in deep time to broadcast a global wake up call, or the human species could go the way of the Dodo bird.

You also understand that although *we* must do this – whatever "this" turns out to be – you've decided that *you* must do this. It's a *hot eagle moment.* That's another new term of mine. Going "hot eagle" is the opposite of going "cold turkey." It describes total, passionate, 100% commitment.

I am living on Maui and become ill. My naturopathic doctor calls to let me know that my test results are in. She suggests that we meet by the ocean at sunrise.

I endure a sleepless night, fearing the worst. The next morning we meet on the beach at sunrise and she tells me that all is well. A simple remedy will heal me.

In the moment before her reassuring words, while praying for strength to bear the news, I hallucinate three Hawaiian warriors standing on a nearby lava spit. They glare at me and transmit a silent message: "Do what you came here to do, for our tribe!"

I know that it will take the remainder of my life to fully understand this message and complete my mission.

making your contribution

A spiritual seeker asked his master: "How long will it take me to reach enlightenment if I meditate an hour a day?" His teacher replied, "Twenty years." The eager student then asked, "And how long if I meditate four hours a day." His master answered, "Then it would take you sixty years."

So, relax. That character who wants to rush the process is not you.

Here we are, diving into the "doing" part of this book, so let's remind ourselves that there are two ways to do everything: the hard way and the easy way. The easy way is to be pulled by a compelling vision. The hard way is to push towards a goal. What would you prefer? And, what will your contribution be?

As I mentioned earlier, you won't donate to feed a million starving children. You might donate to save Maria. Feeding Maria converts a global crisis into personal action, right here, right now. You write the check, you make a contribution. But that generosity might lapse, unless your desire to contribute is consistently fed by a compelling vision.

Andrew Harvey's system of sacred activism hinges on finding your "heartbreak" and following it to discover your personal cause. One of his own heartbreaks and causes is the inhumane treatment of animals, so he advocates for them. His book, *The Hope,* is a must-read, for fully reclaiming yourself and contributing meaningfully as a quantum activist.

He writes:

> The only questions you will be asked when you cross over the waters of death are "What did you do while the world was burning? How did you work to heal the horror of the world on fire? What did you love enough to risk and give your life for?"Nothing else will matter. Understand this now. Turn away from everything you have been and done and believed, and dive into the furnace of a divine love that embraces all beings. Give your whole life to spread and embody the message of its passion to the world – that the world must now wake up, claim the sacred fire that lives within every human heart, and act from it. The one hope, both for you and for humanity, is to take up the challenge of the divine and put the fire of divine compassion into radical action in every arena of the world. [2]

What's your heartbreak? What's your cause? How will you contribute in this now or never moment on planet earth?

We've been frogs in the warming pan for centuries. So far, we haven't stirred much, let alone jump. It takes something "urgently compelling" to finally make us leap and save ourselves from boiling to death.

Motivation through fear doesn't guarantee ongoing action, by the way, only ongoing fear. There's a more effective long-term motivation: love.

follow your heartbreak

Love will guide you when you follow your heartbreak. You may be led to a book, counsel from a wise elder, a song, a movie, or a dream. You might be called into the forest and, strolling there, "get an idea." Where did that idea come from?

You might find yourself watching the news or reading an article online when you are suddenly moved to tears and some kind of deep understanding dawns: "*This* is what I must devote myself to."

And, with that commitment comes a moment of terrible realization. I remember my moment:

I am stirred to tears by the mess I've helped create on this planet with my apathy and self-preoccupation. I beg forgiveness for every narcissistic moment. But I'm acting now, compelled by the powerful vision of a thriving future for our great grandchildren.

It's late. There is no guarantee we will succeed. In fact, the odds are stacked against us. But we owe it to those future generations to try. Don't we?

Each of us can ask: "What's my contribution going to be?"

another nature inspiration

Don't expect him to pick up a novel anytime soon, but Dan the baboon and five buddies know real English words when they see them. For instance, if Dan sees the letters BRRU, ITCS, and KITE, he'll pick out the last one as the real word, even though he doesn't know what it means," the Associated Press reports. "After doing 300,000 tests in France, the animals were able to pick out real words nearly 75% of the time.

The primates process the words by separating them into parts. They learned, for example, that SH is a legitimate construction, whereas FX isn't. This way of thinking helped them identify words they'd never seen before. What's more, they did the study when they felt like it: If they wanted a reward, they could head to a training station at any time. Not only does the experiment show 'amazing cognitive abilities' among baboons, it also points to an innate sense of pattern that may exist in humans, too. [3]

the urgency of now

We can't wait any longer to restore
our relationship with the Earth
because right now the Earth and everyone on Earth
is in real danger.

When a society is overcome by greed and pride,
there is violence and unnecessary devastation.
When we perpetrate violence
toward our own and other species,
we're being violent toward ourselves at the same time.

When we know how to protect all beings,
we will be protecting ourselves.

A spiritual revolution is needed if we're going to confront
the environmental challenges that face us. [4]

"A spiritual revolution is needed." I agree with Thich Nhat Hanh's words above, and that's what this book is meant to inspire and support. I've made this as urgent as it deserves to be from word one.

guidance

Whatever you are most deeply committed to guides your decisions.

There are those things we must do, should do, want to do, and those things we choose to avoid. We *must* wear clothes in public, drive on the correct side of the road, drink, and eat.

We *should* floss our teeth regularly, remember our husband's (or wife's) birthday, and make dinner for the family.

We *want* what feels good: to love and be loved, to meditate, eat good food, win the game, get the promotion, and be successful.

We *avoid* what we don't want to do: filing our taxes, washing dishes, ironing and vacuuming (revealing my gender here). We substitute habits like watching TV excessively, drinking too much, and faking sick days.

And, of course, we're all different. Some people *must* work out in the gym to feel healthy. Others *must* avoid it at all costs. Some *must* be in a relationship. Others *must* go solo. Some *must* dedicate their lives to a better future of mankind; others *must* hide in distractions.

This comment from the book, *Ecopsychology*, provides some insights.

> The psyche restructures itself to survive. The technological construct erodes primary sources of satisfaction once found routinely in life in the wilds, such as physical nourishment, vital community, fresh food, continuity between work and meaning, unhindered participation in life experiences, personal choices, community decisions, and spiritual connection with the natural world. These are the needs we were born to have satisfied. In the absence of these we will not be healthy. In their absence, bereft and in shock, the psyche finds some temporary satisfaction in pursuing secondary sources like drugs, violence, sex, material possessions, and machines. [5]

The challenge is to give up secondary sources of temporary/immediate gratification and commit to a new primary source: participating in the trim tab to help steer humanity in a healthy new direction.

If we've awakened to the point where we *must* find and follow our calling, *this* is the only thing that can make us truly happy.

happiness

Seeking happiness outside of ourselves is a well-trodden path to disappointment. The constitution may entitle us to "the pursuit of happiness" but The Happy Planet Index ranks America 105th of 151 countries in personal happiness scores. [6] Apparently, not many Americans have caught up with happiness yet. More material pursuit will change nothing; this is a spiritual problem.

A spiritual revolution is required, one that replaces belief-centered, speculative religion that demonizes earthly pleasures (making them ever more attractive) with an earth-centered spirituality that celebrates God-in-matter and champions the enjoyment inherent in being human.

This recalls indigenous values. Note The Indian Ten Commandments: [7]

1. Treat the Earth and all that dwell therein with respect.
2. Remain close to the Great Spirit.
3. Show great respect for your fellow beings.
4. Work together for the benefit of all Mankind.
5. Give assistance and kindness wherever needed.
6. Do what you know to be right.
7. Look after the well-being of Mind and Body.
8. Dedicate a share of your efforts to the greater Good.
9. Be truthful and honest at all times.
10. Take full responsibility for your actions.

Compare those to the Christian Ten Commandments: [8]

1. You shall have no other gods before Me.
2. You shall not make idols.
3. You shall not take the name of the LORD your God in vain.
4. Remember the Sabbath day, to keep it holy.
5. Honor your father and your mother.
6. You shall not murder.
7. You shall not commit adultery.
8. You shall not steal.
9. You shall not bear false witness against your neighbor.
10. You shall not covet.

The differences are profound.

The first four in the Christian version are about worshiping a God of belief. Number six in the Indian version is: "Do what you know to be right." This ability arises not from faith in a God of belief but from connection within the universal rightness of the Divine in form.

Comparing these two documents affords us a clear view of the differences between belief based religion and nature based spirituality. One lives in the head, the other in the world. One commands and controls, the other nurtures.

It's clear which "philosophy" to embrace if we wish to contribute to a new and sustainable culture.

from "must" as duty to "must" as desire

Many contributive behaviors can be motivated by a sense of duty and that's honorable, but they might fail when confronted with doing something overly difficult. The sense of duty might fray enough to quit altogether. Being motivated by duty has finite limits. Knowing that you *should* do something without *wanting* to do it is bound to disintegrate when the going gets sufficiently tough, for all but the super human. We could aspire to be super human, or we could become truly human.

Once you are passionately committed to something or someone, duty dissolves into desire. "I must contribute because it's my duty," becomes "I must contribute because I *want* to."

Finding and following your heartbreak to a personal cause creates commitment. Now you *want* to help. It's personal, it's emotional, it's inside you. Your must/duty has become a must/desire. Now you want to do what's right and you will, because it's become your passion.

Deepening your connection with nature and sustaining a robust spiritual practice helps get you more committed and keeps you there. Likewise, learning how to use tools of transformation helps you stay committed.

It took about two years of research and ritual preparation to arrive at a stormy midnight in the Iao Valley on Maui, ready to create a newmory by completing a past life ceremony interrupted by a fatal knife wound to my back.

Now, a hundred years later, I stand on the same rock, finishing my memorial blessing for the scores of warriors who just died in battle. I invite them to go home.

The valley seems to lighten and my chronic fear of public speaking vanishes immediately, never to return.

famories, newmories, focus

Linear time restricts us to the limitations of a seemingly unchangeable past and an unpredictable future. In a prior chapter you learned about famories and newmories. Practice six, detailed at the end of this chapter, invites you to travel along the linear timeline to heal the past, create the future, and enjoy the present.

As a refresher, a famory is "a future memory that feels familiar." You imagine yourself in the future, reflecting back on a successful outcome. You tune in to how it will feel.

A newmory is a changed memory. You connect with a recollection, identify what was happening, feel it fully, determine what qualities were missing, then transmit those qualities into the memory, transforming it.

Last year I slipped on ice and broke my back. Fortunately, I sustained only two minor fractures; healing was swift and complete.

But the memories of that fall – the excruciating pain and the fear about how much damage might have been done – created waking nightmares. I would suddenly remember the incident and feel terror in my body. That's not healthy, so I created a new memory. Here's the newmory I made:

> *I fly into the air and am caught by two angels who lower me to the best spot for a minor injury. Healing will be fast, with no lingering damage. I am flooded with peace.*

I had to run this new program about 50 times before the memory changed. Now, whenever I remember that injury, I feel peace.

As for the present moment, you've learned about focus proximity. How close or how distant do you need to be from whatever is happening and whoever is here? Learn to focus just right, for maximum power and enjoyment.

Practice Six - Navigation

"I heal the past, create the future, and enjoy the present."

This practice is for navigating your life by living on purpose. You do this by using your quantum skills to heal the past, create the future, and enjoy the present. Also, you develop a life line vision board, as explained on page 86.

The movement is a sense of overflowing energy. "My cup runneth over." The feeling is unlimited creativity. Your image is a clearing demonstration I'll describe here. You *can* try this at home.

Assemble a large bowl, a spoon, a clear drinking glass, a pitcher of water, and a bottle of cola. Place the glass in the bowl and fill it half full of water.

Now, pour the cola to fill up the glass. You'll notice that the originally clear water turns a murky brown.

This symbolically enacts the process of pollution all of us have suffered, living in a toxic world and permeated by negativity from parents, teachers, peers and mass media.

Now try clearing up the polluted water. First, take the spoon and stir. Next, stare at the glass. Finally, talk to it. Notice that nothing changes. In other words, fighting what's wrong doesn't work; talk therapy won't fully heal trauma; merely contemplating a problem doesn't solve it.

Now, pour clear water into the glass and continue as it overflows. Keep pouring. The water eventually returns to clarity.

This symbolizes our generative expression as quantum activists, being the change we wish to see in the world by expressing with clarity those qualities we wish to increase. This also demonstrates a unique way to heal trauma, express what was missing.

We are creative. We experience what we express. Express love and compassion and forgiveness that's the world we create.

࿔

*Both abundance and lack exist simultaneously
in our lives, as parallel realities.
It is always our conscious choice
which secret garden we will tend...
when we choose not to focus on what is missing
from our lives but are grateful
for the abundance that's present
—love, health, family, friends, work,
the joys of nature and personal pursuits
that bring us pleasure —
the wasteland of illusion falls away
and we experience Heaven on earth.*

~ Sarah Ban Breathnach

abundance

*The basic concept in Native American culture is
"You should never own anything
that you couldn't give away.*

~ LaDonna Harris

Attorneys understand that you need to have a good memory when you lie. Likewise, you need to have good defenses when you own. The idea (mentioned above) of never owning anything that we couldn't give away may be our only salvation from the paranoia that accompanies private ownership.

In this chapter I will introduce the concept of abundance as a replacement for scarcity. I will also begin to share my grand vision, because it relates to exactly this.

ownership vs. stewardship

The Native American perspective was that we don't own anything but we are stewards of everything. That could be described in a single word: responsibility.

Ownership is onerous. Interesting how coded our English language is with odd collisions of ironic meaning. *Onerous* is described on Wiki as "burdensome, arduous, strenuous, difficult, hard, severe, heavy, backbreaking, weighty, uphill, challenging, formidable, laborious, herculean, exhausting, tiring, taxing, demanding, punishing, grueling, exacting, wearing, wearisome, and fatiguing."

Sounds like an accurate description of the situation we've gotten ourselves into in the twenty-first century with our ownership economy.

Conversely, stewardship is defined online as "the careful and responsible management of something entrusted to one's care." S

That sounds like a completely different paradigm.

visionary strategies

Shifting paradigms from ownership to stewardship is a key to our human survival. It happens in consciousness, one individual at a time. Here are some clues about the implications, framed as visionary strategies, and beginning with a single question that develops concrete realizations about how abundance populates the paradigm of stewardship.

Who would we need to become to make it as a species,
to successfully navigate the immense challenges
that threaten our survival beyond the twenty-first century?

We would need to reconnect with nature and the Divine and change our thinking from fixing problems to accessing genius, using imagery to grow our visions of a healthy future. That's abundance.

Those visions would be holistic, highly attuned to the intelligence of Gaia herself, fulfilled by utilizing available, renewable resources like other species do but leveraging them how only humans can. That's abundance.

We would abandon ego cleverness to become communal creative artists of life, instinctively doing the right thing, in harmony with all beings. Our will, Divine will — the same. That's abundance.

We would reconnect with our neighbors, human and non-human alike. Our fundamental mindset would shift from independence to interdependence and we would learn how to function synergistically to fulfill larger, sustainable intentions for the wellbeing of kin and environment. That's abundance.

The panic and fear that has generated our addiction to isolated security would dissolve into the comfort of belonging within the web of all life, secure in a new kind of faith that doesn't depend on fortress defenses or religious disempowerment. That's abundance.

"Me" would merge into "we," creating a colorful society fundamentally dissimilar from those grim 1984 depictions of mind-numbed zombies enslaved in a spirit crushing socialist prison complex.

Wealth would no longer be measured in accumulation but in balanced distribution, because the concept of protected private ownership would evolve into trusting, shared stewardship. Instead of *owning* things we would *care for* things and willingly, happily, redistribute excess to balance lack, not because of humanitarian generosity but through common sense.

Success would depend on cooperative teamwork, not on competitive individual manipulations. Our striving to achieve would become interpersonal and the power wielded by a handful of billionaire celebrities would be super-ceded by millions of quantum activists collaborating together. That's abundance.

We would understand and experience deep time — cyclical, not linear — and welcome all the seasons of our lives, enjoying the gestation of winter as much as the hope of spring, the pleasure of summer, and the contemplation of autumn. We would develop patience, and *experience* abundance.

we're not on our own

Michael Pollan, author of The Omnivore's Dilemma, was featured in a number of blogposts that illuminate the amazing abilities of plants. From one of those commentaries:

> Plants can do incredible things. They do seem to remember stresses and events... "They do have the ability to respond to 15-20 environmental variables," (Michael) Pollan says. "The issue is, is it right to call it *learning?* Is that the right word? Is it right to call it *intelligence?* Is it right, even, to call what they are *conscious?* Some of these plant neurobiologists believe that plants are conscious — not self-conscious, but conscious in the sense they know where they are in space ... and react appropriately to their position in space."
>
> Pollan says there is no agreed definition of intelligence. Go to Wikipedia and look up intelligence. They despair of giving you an

answer. They basically have a chart where they give you nine different definitions. And about half of them depend on a brain — they refer to abstract reasoning or judgment,and the other half merely refer to a problem-solving ability. And that's the kind of intelligence we are talking about here. So intelligence may well be a property of life. And our difference from these other creatures may be a matter of difference of degree rather than kind. We may just have more of this problem-solving ability and we may do it in different ways. Pollan says that really freaks people out — "that the line between plants and animals might be a little softer than we traditionally think of it as." He suggests that plants may be able to teach humans a thing or two, such as how to process information without a central command post like a brain. [1]

solving the riddle

It's time to solve our riddle. Here are the 13 clues again. Seeing them together will make it easier to divine the answer, although some of you may have already guessed.

Clue # 1
What is only real when you use it or don't have it?

Clue # 2:
Those who have it can control those who don't.

Clue # 3:
What do adults need but babies don't?

Clue # 4:
What can't we live without that can also sabotage our fulfillment?

Clue # 5:
What is thinner than cardboard, invisible, more powerful than drugs?

Clue # 6:
What is both ancient and modern and often causes problems?

Clue # 7:
What do we exchange with each other every day
that evokes strong emotional responses?

Clue # 8:
Some say it's over-rated but that's because they have plenty of it.

Clue # 9:
What was found in the Great Pyramid that now lives in cyber space?

Clue # 10:
What used to be visible that has become invisible?

Clue # 11:
What requires our agreement to enable it to influence our lives?

Clue # 12:
What moves faster than a speeding bullet that is not Superman?

Clue # 13:
What do we all have the same amount of at birth and death?

money

Yes, the answer is money. I will list the clues again, inserting "money" at the end of each one so you can anchor the connection to every clue.

Clue # 1
What is only real when you use it or don't have it?
MONEY

Clue # 2:
Those who have it can control those who don't.
MONEY

Clue # 3:
What do adults need but babies don't?
MONEY

Clue # 4:
What can't we live without that can also sabotage our fulfillment?
MONEY

Clue # 5:
What is thinner than cardboard, invisible, more powerful than drugs?
MONEY

Clue # 6:
What is both ancient and modern and often causes problems?
MONEY

Clue # 7:
What do we exchange with each other every day that evokes strong emotional responses?
MONEY

Clue # 8:
Some say it's over-rated but that's because they have plenty of it.
MONEY

Clue # 9:
What was found in the Great Pyramid that now lives in cyber space?
MONEY

Clue # 10:
What used to be visible that has become invisible?
MONEY

Clue # 11:
What requires our agreement to enable it to influence our lives?
MONEY

Clue # 12:
What moves faster than a speeding bullet that is not Superman?
MONEY

Clue # 13:
What do we all have the same amount of at birth and death?
MONEY

a new way of measuring wealth

Money began as a measurement of value and has become a value itself, with devastating consequences. "Trillions of dollars sit in offshore bank accounts. 'James Henry, economist and researcher with the Tax Justice Network (TJN), conducted a study of data from the Bank for International Settlements (BIS), the International Monetary Fund (IMF), and several private sector analysts. He found that between $21 trillion and $32 trillion is hidden in offshore accounts.'" [2]

If that seems like a lot, get a load of this: "Just five U.S.-based tech firms — Apple, Microsoft, Google, Cisco Systems and Oracle -— had cash reserves of $430.3 billion at the end of 2014, the vast majority of which were held overseas, according to a new report from Moody's Investors Service." [3]

Meanwhile, America's infrastructure is in serious jeopardy. The American Society of Civil Engineers, rating America's infrastructure on 16 different categories, gives America a D+ on the state of the infrastructure. The report is clear, America's infrastructure is aging, insufficient, and becoming dangerous.

Quoting from that report: "Over two hundred million trips are taken daily across deficient bridges in the nation's 102 largest metropolitan regions. In total, one in nine of the nation's bridges are rated as structurally deficient, while the average age of the nation's 607,380 bridges is currently 42 years." [4]

Can you imagine how a massive transfer of money from offshore,brought back to help America, could defuse this infrastructure time bomb?

Of course, that proposal raises serious questions. People freak out whenever wealth redistribution is mentioned, perhaps recalling the 1917 Revolution in Russia and the horrors of Stalin that followed.

What about taxes? American companies that are holding significant funds offshore who chose to transfer them back would face massive tax bills. That's a primary reason why they don't do it.

This problem is currently being debated, with plans proposed to close the corporate loopholes that enable American companies to avoid taxes by hoarding funds offshore in the first place.

I predict that will fail, because they are among the ones doing it. Clearly there's greed in this picture, and mistrust. Given government inefficiency and deceit, who would feel confident to pass along more wealth when what's in hand is being so horribly wasted?

I'm no economist and that gives me an advantage. Unburdened by the curse of knowledge, not blinded by precedents, unconcerned about jeopardizing my reputation or offending donors, I can think outside the box.

The real problem, looking from upstream where causes live, is a fundamental misunderstanding and erroneous programming concerning how we define wealth. At the moment wealth = accumulation. We measure what a person owns, what is under their personal control. This can't do anything but lead to hoarding. First you get it (as much as possible), then you try to keep it (as much as possible).

What if we measured wealth in degrees of distribution? The more wealth a person was distributing the wealthier they would be considered.

The first step towards this reframe is to lose our sticky fingers. More (money) is not necessarily better, not when we use a distribution model that measures wealth as balance.

The most obvious example is the human body. There is always good circulation in a healthy body. Blood, nutrients, nerve impulses, etc. Everything moves. In fact, stagnation is a serious medical problem. Water retention (edema), constipation, a sluggish metabolism, all indicating poor circulation.

A problem in one part of the body affects the entire system.
Too bad we don't understand that this same principle
applies just as rigorously to our economic health.

---

new monetary systems

Way back in the introduction I mentioned the healing center I founded in Victoria, BC, Canada and ran for five plus years during the Eighties. We offered our services from a medical dental building downtown and never charged fees. Clients chose what to pay.

We always covered our bills, including my full time salary. Did I get rich? Yes and no. The money was minimal. But we exchanged other forms of wealth as well, and I learned to value and trust a flow of currency beyond the exchange of money. I witnessed the generosity our novel system inspired. I don't recall any of our clients ever being cheap, trying to get a deal.

I do remember clients happily leaving what they could afford and what they decided our services were worth. It was always enough to cover other clients who paid less. It all balanced out over the years and we had no financial problems. In fact, I can't remember ever worrying or talking about money very much. The fear with systems like this is that someone will take advantage. I can only recall one or two people leaving nothing and they never returned, because they didn't value what they received.

Decades later, here in Ashland, Oregon, a friend and I co-founded a Time Exchange program. Six years down the road we have over four hundred members exchanging everything from computer repairs to airport runs, gardening, haircuts, and business coaching.

At the moment we are retooling it to solve various problems that have developed but members agree the system provides a vital service in our community, especially for the elderly and those on a tight budget. Members also use the exchanges to make new friends and deepen their sense of tribal belonging.

from small beginnings ...

There are hundreds of operational exchanges in America and thousands throughout the world. Real services are given and received, largely without any money changing hands. The most significant result is the radical increase in generosity that participants experience.

Sticky fingers give way to trusting hearts.

Even so, I witness scarcity thinking cropping up and have concluded that for significant transformation around money to happen on any scale the kind of inner work this book advocates is unrealistic. Consciousness must change, to create a different reflection in the material world.

This reminds me of something I used to do during workshops. I'd take out a shaver and hand mirror and begin to shave the mirror. It didn't change my face, as puzzled audience members could easily confirm. My point? We can try to manipulate a reflection, or we can work on the original and change the reflection that way.

theory vs. reality

Many years ago I wrote for the Russian comedian Yakov Smirnoff. I only remember a few of his jokes; this was my favorite.

An American and a Russian are talking.

"Tell me how communism works," the American asks. "Well," the Russian replies, "if I had two houses and you had none I would give you one."

"Really? Amazing. And, if you had two cars and I didn't have one, would you give me one of your cars?"

"Absolutely. That's how we share in our country."

"Amazing! So, if you had two chickens would you give me one?

"No."

The American is surprised. "Why not?

"Because I *have* two chickens."

That's the difference between theory and reality. Regarding money, who willingly surrenders funds when the primary gain is social, not personal? Actually, many of us already do that. Still, trillions of dollars sit hoarded in offshore accounts. What would it take to dislodge that stagnation?

Political insiders claim those funds will never move and that encourages me because they are dead wrong so often. Regardless of their cynicism and my naiveté, I've constructed my famory and begun streaming.

I'm imagining how it will feel when that abundance is flowing freely within our monetary system. I see bridges and roads repaired, water systems cleaned up, social services bolstered and homeless people cared for. And, it feels fantastic.

Many of us have a love hate relationship with money. We need it but we also know the misery it can cause, how much human suffering results from greed and poverty. You may have heard the joke: "You can tell what God thinks about money by seeing who he gives most of it to."

I'm not demonizing money and I'm not proposing an alternate paper currency, not even the exchange of hours, such as we use in our local time co-op.

I *am* championing generosity and abundance.

considering an alternative

Years of experience have proven to me that there already *is* another currency and it's not some alternative that we invented. It's the currency that pre-dates money, which I call Love. When people exchange anything with each other voluntarily and with a generous spirit, they are really exchanging Love.

> *The perversion of money from a measurement of value to value in itself has rendered transactions impersonal, lacking in generosity and love. You give me this and I just pay you. We don't have to connect as friends. It's just business. The most graphic example is prostitution, where "love" is traded for money, not voluntarily exchanged for more love.*

Love in its fullness – which is much more than romance – *is* the primary creating currency in the world at large and, I believe, the whole universe. After all, Love – by whatever name – does run the universe. That big Love is creative beyond anything we can accomplish with money. The phrase, "for love or money" suggests the two are mutually exclusive. In fact, they belong together: love *and* money.

Our civilized world runs primarily on the fuel of money; the natural world runs wholly on Love. The result? Ours is a civilization of deceit funded by the misuse of money. Nature remains a community of collaborators sustained by the innate fairness of love. Yes, creatures eat each other but that's a necessary feature of survival. Irrational greed and hatred, I propose, are human traits.

To merely fight the money system is to increase conflict. Whistleblowers discover this. If they expose the truth about money they could become fugitives or go to jail. No wonder. Nothing threatens the stability of our society like challenging the currency that runs it. Of course, behind the misuse of money is a chronically dysfunctional way of thinking, ingrained in us from birth. Changing that mindset is where quantum activists focus, with appreciation for those in the trenches advocating for change.

We can't change mindsets by force or decree. Especially today, where the long standing misuse of money has corrupted our understanding of "value" to such an extent that most people can't even conceive of a workable alternative.

To suggest relinquishing our grip on this devastatingly destructive, dysfunctional, chronically unfair system, reminds me of the story about how they catch monkeys in India. They place a banana in a small bottle and wait for a monkey to discover it. He reaches inside and grabs the banana but can't remove his hand unless he lets go. But he won't let go.

Instead, he submits to capture and loses his life. This is an apt analogy for how we cling to money. There are trillions of bananas grasped oversees while the demise of our economic system accelerates.

Who's going to let go?

the biggest elephant

When it comes to money, we just don't see the obvious problem, "the elephant in the room." In America that elephant is the Federal Reserve. It's not federal and there are no reserves. Federal Reserve banks are private corporations and the Fed prints money for the government. The government could print its own money but it doesn't. Instead, it pays face value for paper money and interest on the debt. The government could print our money but doesn't. It once did, twice actually.

In the first case, "President Lincoln printed 400 million dollars worth of Greenbacks (the exact amount being $449,338,902), money that he delegated to be created, a debt-free and interest-free money to finance the (Civil) War. It served as legal tender for all debts, public and private. He printed it, paid it to the soldiers, to the U.S. Civil Service employees, and bought supplies for war.

"Shortly after that happened, 'The London Times' printed the following: 'If that mischievous financial policy, which had its origin in the North American Republic, should become indurated down to a fixture, then that Government will furnish its own money without cost. It will pay off debts and be without a debt. It will have all the money necessary to carry on its commerce. It will become prosperous beyond precedent in the history of the civilized governments of the world. The brains and the wealth of all countries will go to North America. That government must be destroyed, or it will destroy every monarchy on the globe.'" [5]

President Lincoln was assassinated.

"On June 4th, 1963, President Kennedy signed a presidential document, called Exec-utive Order 11110, which further amended Executive Order 10289 of September 19th, 1951. This gave Kennedy, as President of the United States, legal clearance to create his own money to run the country, money that would belong to the people, an Interest and debt-free money. He had printed United States Notes, completely ignoring the Federal Reserve Notes from the private banks of the Federal Reserve." [6]

President Kennedy was assassinated.

Many years earlier, around 1750, Benjamin Franklin wrote about life in the early colonies. This was long before there was a central bank in America like the one in England that the Pilgrims had fled.

> There was abundance in the Colonies, and peace was reigning on every border. It was difficult, and even impossible to find a happier and more prosperous nation on all the surface of the globe. Comfort was prevailing in every home. The people, in general, kept the highest moral standards, and education was widely spread." [7]

Franklin made a trip to England and was shocked to discover their working population in abject poverty. The elite there inquired of Franklin what their secret was in the Colonies. He replied: "We have no poor houses in the Colonies; and if we had some, there would be nobody to put in them, since there is, in the colonies, not a single unemployed person, neither beggars nor tramps."

Why the difference? He explained: "In the Colonies, we issue our own paper money. It is called 'Colonial Scrip.' We issue it in proper proportion to make the goods pass easily from the producers to the consumers. In this manner, creating ourselves our own paper money, we control its purchasing power and we have no interest to pay to no one."

Note something highly significant in what Benjamin Franklin reported: "goods pass easily from the producers to the consumers." There's no mention of a middle-man in there. The central bank, the financial industry, *are* the middle man. If we really want to make America great again, we'd have to rewind to a time before the implementation of that enslaving construct or establish a new system not run by private bankers.

the wisdom of love

Speaking of insanity, near the end of the 1966 film, *King of Hearts*, Alan Bates's character is searching frantically to find and defuse a time bomb that will blow up everyone in their small French village at midnight. Meanwhile, Genevieve Bujold's character just wants to make out.

Here's what I remember happened. He wards her off repeatedly, finally exploding in frustration: "Don't you know that we only have five minutes left?" She batts her long eyelashes, pulls him close, and whispers, "Five minutes would be wonderful!" He lets go into her arms and relaxes. The currency of Love flows freely. Moments later, he jumps up and exclaims, "Aha! I know where the bomb is!"

He saves the town and gets the girl. What made the difference? What enabled him to figure out where the bomb was? Not money. Love, the power of Love. The following metaphor will explain how this works.

Imagine a bell in a jar. The jar is airtight and attached to a pump, which fills the jar with air. When you press a button the bell chimes, loud and strong. Now, you flip a switch to reverse the pump and suck air out of the jar. The volume of the bell gradually diminishes, fading into silence as a vacuum is created.

Sound waves can't transmit in a vacuum. You know that bell is still ringing but you can't hear it until you reverse the pump again and return air to the jar. Then the bell gradually becomes audible again.

Meaning: we always need a medium to transmit a message.

The bell needs air to be heard. Bates's character needed Love to perceive. In the commercial world, we need money to transmit value. But money is just the medium, it's not the value itself. Except, that's what its become.

So, what value are we transmitting through money? What value *could* we transmit through money?

pneumaplasm

I learned the term "pneumaplasm" (spirit substance) when I was studying energy medicine in the seventies and eighties. I was heartened to find the word still in use today and to locate the following lengthy articulation from an old friend of mine, Jerry Kvasnica, who artfully describes this essential substance and illuminates what we can transmit through money.

... it is universally acknowledged that money has no intrinsic value, that it is merely paper and serves only as a medium of exchange. Of what is money the medium? What does it represent? Ultimately and ideally money represents life itself. Whatever increases or facilitates the flow of life on Earth has value or, as I like to think of it, substance. An ear of corn grown by a farmer obviously has substance. It *is* substance. Because this substance has the capacity to sustain life when it is consumed by human beings or livestock, it has value. The farmer who, along with nature, assists in the generation of this substance is entitled to compensation in money commensurate with the value of the substance.

This is a very simple example having to do with a tangible commodity. The corn can be seen and touched, but a great deal of substance generation is intangible. The waitress who serves the corn to a customer in a restaurant has not actually produced anything physical. But in offering a service that in essence facilitates the flow of life, she has generated substance, something that has value in monetary terms. The substance itself is invisible but is nevertheless very real and merits compensation.

Ideas represent an even more subtle level of substance generation. Merely by conceiving of a new way of doing things or a new device for doing things, an individual may generate substance, provided the idea when implemented will enhance rather than dissipate the quality of life on Earth.

The most refined substance generation occurs at the spiritual level. Worship and meditation, to the degree that these are free of religious beliefs and concepts, generate a purity of spiritual substance that I refer to as "pneumaplasm."

In actual fact all substance originates at this level, and substance generated at the physical and mental levels is just a denser form of pneumaplasm. This spirit-substance connects spirit with form, essence with existence, heaven with earth, God with creation. It is the mechanism by which all life on the planet —indeed in the whole universe — is sustained and is the repository of all value.

Pneumaplasm is sacred, and money, when it's allowed to flow in accordance with pneumaplasmic generation, is also sacred. But when human beings act out of ignorance and greed and attempt to manipulate this flow to suit their own purposes, the whole process is profaned and polluted. All money is tainted as a result, and some of this filthy residue inevitably attaches to those who use it.

In view of this and the current dysfunctional state on Earth, we might recognize the wisdom of not accumulating a lot of money. Could it be that those who value frugality and pursue modest lifestyles are, whether they realize it or not, pursuing a very sensible course?" [8]

manipulation or value

This author defines value as "offering a service that in essence facilitates the flow of life generating substance, something that has value in monetary terms." Instantly, we can understand the fatal flaw in our twenty-first century, money-based economy: manipulation.

We have hordes of clever people manipulating money to increase how much they – or their clients, family, and friends – have of it, without necessarily generating any substance of value. Think hedge fund managers, hostile takeovers, and IPO's. Today's financial experts understand how to increase *perceived* value, without increasing *actual* value.

No further "substance" is generated buying low and selling high. It doesn't produce extra corn, to go back to that example. No waitresses have served more people. No value has been created, only the perception of value. Worse, that perceived value has been converted into dollars and sucked out of the system, often stored in offshore accounts.

This is a clever recipe for excess and scarcity, not balance. By the way, virtually nothing has been done to change business-as-usual since the 2008 collapse in the American economy so we can certainly count on more bubble bursting.

Without fundamentally altering the way we define and use money – to *measure* value, not to *be* value – we doom ourselves to boom and bust cycles that will continue to enrich the elite and impoverish the rest of us. I read somewhere that there have been over a dozen boom/bust cycles in the U.S economy over the past 80 years. At some point, the *whole* system must collapse. We may be nearing that point.

love and money

What if we could use money as a medium to transmit Love? How might we do that? Here are a few ideas:

- ☑ Mark the moment money passes from your hand to another's. Consciously let go. Willingly and gladly give what you have; increase your wealth with what you have received, rather than feeling poorer because of what you have lost.

- ☑ Pause to appreciate the service you just received as you fill out a check. Write "thank you" in the memo field.

- ☑ Give more. Surprise a vendor by adding to your bill, if you feel their work has been exemplary. It's bound to stimulate an interesting conversation.

- ☑ Give money away. Carry a bill around with you — a five, ten, twenty, fifty, hundred — and give it to strangers or friends. The amount doesn't matter; it's the principle. I've done this and it's a blast! In fact, I gave away a Benjamin a couple of months ago and it felt marvelous.

- ☑ Change your spending patterns. For instance, you could exchange several expensive designer coffees a week for donations to homeless people, or save up for a few months and surprise your wife with lunch and flowers.

- ☑ Return your own hoarded money back into system and inspire others to do the same on a much bigger scale. Replace fear (saving for a rainy day) with trust (we'll all help each other when the rains come).

I'm a twenty-four-year-old eager beaver with big ideas. The Canadian government offers free business consulting to young entrepreneurs. The counselor who sees me is dour and negative. He rains on my parade and discourages me from proceeding to launch. I listen, he makes good points, but it's disappointing.

I notice how unhappy he seems. As I leave his office, I reach into my pocket and extract the fifty dollar bill I always carry for opportunities just like this.

"Here," I say, extending the bill in his direction. "I like to give money to strangers," I explain. He literally jumps out of his seat and backs away. "Oh, no, that wouldn't be appropriate," he insists. He's afraid this is a bribe but I assure him that I don't want anything in return.

After a few minutes of comical reverse haggling, he finally accepts my gift. And... he completely changes.

He follows me out of his office, stands waiting for the elevator with me, we ride down together, and he walks out onto the street where we stand in the rain as he excitedly tells me about his electric train set and how he will buy a new engine with this fifty dollars.

A grim old man has disappeared and an eager youngster has taken his place. I walk away glowing, thinking, "That's the real power of money!"

money as a benevolent trojan horse

The bell-in-a-jar metaphor demonstrated how we always need a medium to transmit a message. Money is a medium currently used to transmit fear, greed, scarcity, desire, etc. How do you feel when you're paying bills or when you realize you have an unexpected major expense, for example when your car suddenly breaks down?

You can learn how to change those knee-jerk reactions and begin using the medium of money to transmit generosity, love, wealth, and trust. You handle money every day, so you have ongoing opportunities. Every touch is a chance to imbue money with whatever qualities you choose. Who knows where your money will go? Perhaps into the hands of a billionaire. You may never talk to that person but you *can* influence him or her through the money you both touch.

We can use money to reach anyone anywhere who is also using money, and that includes just about everyone. Those more closely attuned to the specific frequency of whatever qualities we are imbuing into our personal money exchanges may sense it on an unconscious level and find themselves spontaneously becoming more generous. What if?

Remember The Hundredth Monkey Phenomenon? Here's an opportunity to stimulate new behaviors (not causing monkeys to wash their potatoes, but inspiring humans to be generous with money), using a technique that doesn't cost a cent or a minute of extra time.

Love using money
and use money
to transmit love.

Help grow the money revolution. We don't have to start it; it's incubating throughout the world in time banks, in cooperative businesses, non-profits and not-for-profit enterprises of all kinds, in communities using alternate currencies, and between neighbors who are giving generously to each other, exchanging love in every transaction.

Become an early adopter and help spread the new habit.

abundance as the norm

We live in an abundant universe. The fact that we have created a scarcity bubble to hide in is not something to be proud of.

Bubbles burst. The scarcity bubble bursts at the moment of death, ironically, in the same moment that we lose everything we own. I wonder if that's something worth paying attention to?

The Biblical injunction, "It's easier for a camel to pass through the eye of the needle than for a rich man to enter the kingdom of God" is interpreted in several ways. There are stories about a gate called The Needle's Eye in ancient Jerusalem, described as small and low. If a camel was to go through, it had to kneel and have its baggage removed.

There's no credible evidence that such a gate ever existed, regardless of how often the story is repeated in Sunday Schools. The Needle's Eye is also supposedly the name of an old mountain pass, narrow enough to force travelers to dismount and rendering them fair game for robbers in hiding.

The principle I extract here relates to humility and the relinquishing of earthly treasures, in order to pass through a portal into another realm. This is exactly what the paradigm shift from scarcity to abundance, from ownership to stewardship, requires:

1. **Humility** – I am not measured by what I own but by who I am and how I behave.

2. **Wealth** – I distribute what I generate, leaving no excess to burden myself with that would prevent experiencing the sheer enjoyment of voluntary generosity.

ॐ

It is the heart that makes a man rich.
He is rich according to what he is,
not according to what he has.

~ Henry Ward Beecher

ॐ

b.h.a.g.

Never surrender your hopes and dreams
to the fateful limitations others have placed on their own lives. The
vision of your true destiny does not reside
within the blinkered outlook of the naysayers
and the doom prophets. Judge not by their words,
but accept advice based on the evidence of actual results.

Do not be surprised should you find a complete absence
of anything mystical or miraculous in the manifested reality
of those who are so eager to advise you.

Friends and family who suffer the lack of abundance,
joy, love, fulfillment and prosperity in their own lives
really have no business imposing their self-limiting beliefs
on your reality experience.

~ Anthon St. Maarten

I work with many famories every day. My big one is a new economy based on the primary currency of Love rather than the substitute currency of money, a stewardship culture rather than an ownership culture.

Author Jim Collins calls a big vision like this a B.H.A.G. – a Big Hairy Audacious Goal.[1] To qualify as a B.H.A.G., a vision must be grandiose, impractical, impossible, and promise enough incredible benefits to compel a person to stick with it through to some degree of success.

Collins wrote that we have to give up good to become great. Let's assume that most of us *are* good. We may have good lives, but they have likely settled into predictable patterns, "comfort zones." Giving up good means risking the loss of comfort in order to become great.

Humanity is languishing in a comfort zone that is increasingly uncomfortable, forging ahead at full speed like the Titanic did, heading for a lethal iceberg of some kind. "Good" keeps us moving towards a date with disaster; "great" changes our direction.

creating your b.h.a.g.

Creating your own B.H.A.G. declares your intention to benefit the world in some grand way. Your personal example can inspire others to do the same. If enough of us do that together, the trim tab can turn the ship.

The poet Rumi wrote:

> There is one thing in this world you must never forget to do. If you forget everything else and not this, there's nothing to worry about, but if you remember everything else and forget this, then you will have done nothing in your life.

> It is as if a king has sent you to a country to do some particular task and you go to that country and perform a hundred other services, but you forget to do the one he sent you to do. All human beings have been sent to this world on a particular mission and that mission is our singular purpose. If we do not enact it we have done nothing." [2]

Focusing and developing my money initiative by broadcasting generosity is the one thing I must do. What's yours?

an economic security blanket

My "must do" is to develop a new experience of wealth and my target is money hoarding. My goal is to liberate the monetary excess that has been siphoned out of the world economy, trillions of dollars that rots in offshore accounts, and to attract that wealth back into the system. I believe that any sort of substantial rebalancing of wealth could work miracles on the planet. Here's a blogger's perspective on the situation:

> Forty percent of the assets of the wealthy are sitting in deposits: the rich person's equivalent of stuffing money into a mattress. Money sitting in deposits in Swiss and Cayman Islands accounts is essentially wasted wealth. It does as little for the economy as

gold hoarded by a dragon in Middle Earth. It essentially sits there uselessly as an economic security blanket for the very people who need it least. [3]

What intelligent person would imagine that hoarding could do anything but harm the world economy? Buried wealth extracts value from the system and that hurts everyone, even those doing the hoarding, although they may be blind to it.

entraining generosity

My favorite Jesus story is the one about the loaves and fishes.

The way the Bible tells it, this was a genuine miracle. Loaves and fishes multiplied magically until everyone had plenty to eat. Where did this abundance of food come from? Jesus somehow increased the little that was there. That does sound like a miracle. Here's a more pragmatic explanation that seems even more inspiring:

Imagine you're heading into the desert with a crowd. You wouldn't know how long you'd be out there so you'd probably pack some water and food. But you might not be sure that everyone else thought to do that. So, you might hide what you had, fearing that if you brought it out to share then you wouldn't have enough left for yourself and your family.

Jesus inspired generosity. He encouraged everyone to share what they had and it turned out that there was plenty for everyone. The appearance of scarcity vanished into the reality of abundance.

This perfectly describes the financial realty of our society today, where there *is* enough for everyone. Could we do as Jesus did and somehow inspire generosity, but with money instead of food?

hoarding

We have to start with ourselves. What are *we* hoarding? What are you hoarding? What am I hoarding? Note: obsessive hoarding is fundamentally different from prudent saving.

We hoard because we are afraid. F.E.A.R. stands for "false expectations appearing real." Like, the fear of not having enough money. What could replace fear? Love, defined as the power that runs the universe.

Some economists conjecture that a fair distribution of wealth would render everyone poor. I scoured the literature to confirm or dispute this fear, got a headache from conflicting reports, and am no closer to a verifiable answer. But the concept exposes the bankruptcy of civilization. Nature shares resources without measuring a single exchange ... and nature is not going broke!

dreaming a new economy

The problems in our money-based economy are complex but they are not unsolvable. What if we used our imagination? Within imagination, we can develop a multitude of solutions to contemplate and refine until we're ready to launch a sound strategy in the real world for careful testing. I know there are very smart people working on this right now.

> *Imagine a municipality having funds to fix a bridge, clean up their water system, renovate the fire station, buy new trucks, and hire local people. Imagine businesses benefiting from those improvements. Imagine senior citizens being able to babysit their grandchildren instead of working at Walmart. Imagine compassionate health care, nutritious lunches for school children, and well-paid teachers with smaller classes.*

On and on it goes. In fact, it's truly mind boggling to contemplate the economic impact of returning hoarded trillions to our economy. Wait — I know — it would take a lot more than just bringing back the cash and giving it away. We would need responsible stewards of those funds and a new system, and before that, a transformation in consciousness around money itself. That's where quantum activists come in.

what goes around comes around

Ironically, transferred money from offshore accounts — where it generates more money in the form of interest — could eventually recirculate back to the wealthy through the businesses they developed to generate those funds in the first place.

Why then wouldn't they infuse the economy with their hoarded funds, welcome those funds returning to them, and keep them circulating over and over again for everyone's benefit? Probably because they're sure someone else would hoard it once they let go. One banana in hand is considered worth more than many on the tree, even if it leads to death (for a monkey trapped by his hunger).

I'm not proposing a socialist seizure of wealth. I'm imagining those who have too much sharing with those who have too little in order to create financial balance for all. Any initiative like that would have to be entirely voluntary down to the smallest and largest transactions.

This may sound impossible but urgent times call for radical solutions. We simply *can't* continue doing what we've been doing in our economy and in every other aspect of twentieth-century society and expect different results. Business-as-usual has no future. Anyone who thinks my idea stinks and has a zero chance of happening, please tell me about your better idea. I'm hopeful and confident that there are already a *thousand* good ideas that we can celebrate together in 2025.

Why might the super rich consider my idea? Is it because they are humanitarian? Maybe yes, but probably not. More likely, it's because they become inspired to generosity. They might come to realize the insanity of greed and excess.

Remember my description of how the body shares resources? Imagine this body talk:

> *"So, my left foot needs blood? Forget about it. What did my left foot ever do to deserve more blood? I'll just keep as much blood as I can stored in my heart... oh, wait, what's that bursting feeling?"*

Is it possible that the excessively rich could be touched by the Hundredth Monkey transmissions of ordinary people like us who infuse generosity and trust and Love in the money we distribute, so that they *want* to participate? Obviously, this must start and continue on the local level. Where are the financial needs in our communities and where is the hoarded wealth? We can start small and build examples of economic success to inspire others.

That's exactly how Jesus worked that miracle with the loaves and fishes. I doubt that he wrote a white paper or launched a media campaign. He simply entrained others into a spontaneous expansion of trust and generosity. His living example catalyzed that miracle. Our turn.

You're not Jesus and neither am I, but we have our own opportunities to inspire and entrain others and we *are* handling money every day.

We're connected with each other through our money exchanges, whether we're moving paper or making digital transfers. This gives us opportunities every day, not just once in the desert.

your turn

I just invested a few pages to communicate about my project. This is meant to help you imagine yours. So, it's time now to find *your* cause.

Will you follow your heartbreak to discover your own B.H.A.G.? Will you embrace your own "now or never moment" and commit? Will you become part of the trim tab and help steer humanity in new directions? Will you be able to honestly say, as Bucky did, "Call me trim tab?"

Here are some ideas to stimulate your imagination. Notice, I'm inserting a question mark (?) for the goals. Measurable goals are essential and for B.H.A.G.'s they must be outrageously ambitious and seemingly impossible; like putting a man on the moon and bringing him back safely, thanks to JFK.

1. **Healthy Children**: Reduce the number of poor and starving children from 795 million (one in nine) to ? by May 1, 2025.

2. **Safety for Women**: Ensure that women feel as safe as men. Eliminate rape and sexual abuse and decrease global incidents to ? by May 1, 2025.

3. **Child Abuse**: Transform the cultural norms, particularly in organized religion. Decrease child abuse to ? by May 1, 2025.

4. **Rain Forest Protection**: Ensure that rain forests are protected and that they reach sustainability through sane harvesting and reforestation by May 1, 2025.

5. **Health Care**: Guarantee truly affordable health care for every U.S. resident within a not-for-profit health care system by May 1, 2025.

All of these probably seem impossible. That's one of the pre-requisites for a worthwhile B.H.A.G. Now, study your lifeline vision board to discern the patterns in your life. Consider the world scene complete with so many crises, and ask yourself, "What breaks my heart?" Think as big as you can. Discover what your B.H.A.G. initiative could be.

You will know when you've got it because you will feel it living inside you. Remember Michelangelo? The statue of David lived in him. What Michelangelo did was reveal what was already there. It wasn't just in the stone, it was in him. He had to first embody the art within himself, not just create it outside himself. This is what quantum activists do. Let's help each other make our B.H.A.G.'s real "out there" because we start by making them real "in here."

I hope you will recommend this book to friends who are already roaring along with their own big social change initiatives. We all know a few of those exceptional individuals. It will encourage them to know they are about to have more company. Let's see who all we can invite to the party on May 1, 2025.

ॐ

*The real voyage of discovery
consists not in seeking new landscapes,
but in having new eyes.*

~ Marcel Proust

discovery

*The beginning of knowledge
is the discovery of something
we do not understand.*

~ Frank Herbert

Meditation used to be some weird thing they did in India. Now it's become commonplace in millions of Western lives. Credit the Maharishi and The Beatles for helping meditation go mainstream.

The next practice to gain traction is called Mindfulness, defined this way by Jon Kabat Zinn, the founder of Mindfulness-Based Stress Reduction: "Mindfulness is awareness that arises through paying attention, on purpose, in the present moment, non-judgmentally. It's about knowing what is on your mind." [1]

I predict that mindfulness will take its place alongside meditation as a broadly accepted and extremely helpful mainstream practice. What's next? My vote goes to the concept of "discovery." It seems a natural next step and here's the progression:

1. **You meditate**, retreating from the busyness of the day to connect with Love and feel the peace and contentment that arises from belonging in the flow of life force.

2. **You become mindful**, expanding that meditative state beyond a disciplined, eyes-closed meditation, to become more fully present, focusing your thoughts.

3. **You discover** what you can learn in the moment, accessed through a meditative inner state plus the habit of mindfulness.

We've been exercising our capacity for discovery throughout this book. Early on, I suggested that we become detectives of life, following the clues that present themselves day-to-day, to access the genius of life that can show up in many forms, internal and external.

Good detectives ignore nothing. They don't discard information that doesn't, for the moment, make sense or conform to their way of thinking. They succeed by expecting the unexpected, seeing through illusion to glimpse hidden truths, discovering what's *really* going on, while surrounded by those who have discounted clues that don't conform to their fixed mindsets.

dreaming 2025

We've got years ahead of us (as of this writing) to discover and activate our B.H.A.G.'s en route to a rendezvous with each other in 2025.

Again, we may cringe at the grandiosity. But remember the power of intention. Making a commitment unleashes powerful forces. It's how we create even the most unlikely, impossible, future.

We're learning how to live on purpose. Having a BIG purpose is vital. Obviously, we can't get hung up on achieving precise results. We don't control the universe! But intention and commitment attract support. All kinds of miracles can occur when we tap into that magic.

> *It's May 1, 2025.*
>
> *I'm celebrating with friends, aware of New World parties around the world, a world that is being transformed.*
>
> *The economy now supports those with less; balance is growing. We are successfully coping with environmental challenges.*
>
> *I feel uplifted, validated, ecstatic, luminous, and I'm overflowing with appreciation for every individual who helped this dream come true.*
>
> *My mind reflects on the many initiatives I am aware of: feeding children, protecting the weak, caring for our environment, using innovative technologies that advance civilization without destroying us.*
>
> *A clarion declaration echoes through my mind: "We did it!"*

This chapter is short by design. I expect it will lengthen dramatically as B.H.A.G.'s come to my attention and I submit revised manuscripts (self publishing is great, you can update the text whenever you wish).

Let me know about your B.H.A.G. Email to will@willtwilkinson.com and visit my site for news of what others are doing around the world: www.willtwilkinson.com.

Let's use this new practice I'm advocating – discovery – to co-create a future that our great grandchildren deserve.

৵

How should we be able to forget those ancient myths
that are at the beginning of all peoples,
the myths about dragons that at the last moment
turn into princesses;
perhaps all the dragons of our lives are princesses
who are only waiting to see us once beautiful and brave.
Perhaps everything terrible is in its deepest being
something helpless that wants help from us.

So you must not be frightened if a sadness rises up
before you larger than any you have ever seen;
if a restiveness, like light and cloud shadows,
passes over your hands and over all you do.

You must think that something is happening with you,
that life has not forgotten you, that it holds you in its hand;
it will not let you fall. Why do you want to shut out of your life
any uneasiness, any miseries, or any depressions?

For after all, you do not know what work these conditions
are doing inside you.

~ Rainer Maria Rilke

transmission

As we live, we are transmitters of life.
And when we fail to transmit life, life fails to flow through us.

That is part of the mystery of sex, it is a flow onwards.
Sexless people transmit nothing.

And if, as we work, we can transmit life into our work,
life, still more life, rushes into us to compensate, to be ready
and we ripple with life through the days.

Even if it is a woman making an apple dumpling,
or a man a stool,
if life goes into the pudding, good is the pudding
good is the stool,
content is the woman, with fresh life rippling in to her,
content is the man.

Give, and it shall be given unto you
is still the truth about life.
But giving life is not so easy.
It doesn't mean handing it out to some mean fool,
or letting the living dead eat you up.
It means kindling the life-quality where it was not,
even if it's only in the whiteness of a washed pocket-handkerchief.

~ D. H. Lawrence

B.H.A.G.'s are big change initiatives. How will they succeed? Let's ask Mother. In other words, how does change happen in nature? Osmosis is one way, which Wiki describes as "The spontaneous net movement of solvent molecules through a semi-permeable membrane into a region of higher solute concentration, in the direction that tends to equalize the solute concentrations on the two sides." [1]

Osmosis occurring between humans is called entrainment, a natural process that is happening right now between you and me as I write and you read. Hopefully, this makes sense, with your new understanding of deep time. We are writing and reading together, in a dimension beyond linear time and geography, bonded by our voluntary attention.

A peculiar kind of transmission is occurring through an imbalance between us. Something in me has risen to be articulated in words. They cast their spell. Something in you has risen to welcome these words. They have called to you and you have answered. Here you are, reading.

The phrase, "When the student is ready the teacher appears" only begins to explain this phenomenon; it doesn't tell the whole story. For one thing, the teaching goes both ways. In these moments of our writing/reading we are communing soul to soul and I am learning too.

the secret of spelling

True teaching is more than imparting knowledge as a one-way transmission, it's a holistic exchange not limited to just us. We learn to transmit together, to access genius together, within the quantum field. In the process, we forge a learning relationship, fundamentally different from top-down, knowledge-based teaching that increases and maintains separation between the one who "knows" and the one who doesn't. That is a one-way transaction based in superior/inferior disconnection.

Osmosis learning, which I call "mutual entrainment," flows both ways, dissolving boundaries and increasing connection. Such an exchange is occurring between us right now. In the same moments that you are being affected by my writing, I am being influenced by your attention on the words I wrote. This is the multi-dimensional secret of spelling, the word we use to describe the correct formation of words. Words cast spellings. Spells make magic.

The book of John in the Bible begins: "In the beginning was the Word, and the Word was with God, and the Word was God." Maybe that gives us a clue about the importance of words.

Words matter... in ways we may not have consciously acknowledged.

entrainment

Something flows between us, enters us, and begins to live in us through our interaction. This may sound exotic, but we've all experienced it many times. Someone is excited about their new Mac and we suddenly begin to think about getting one too, not because we were logically persuaded but because we got caught up in their "reality warp field." A friend raves about a movie and we want to see it. Another friend champions a restaurant, a book, an event. Enthusiasm is contagious.

What resonates between two or more people also radiates beyond them. Our shared transmission moves out like the ripples in a pond when a pebble drops. This is the catalyst that engineers The Hundredth Monkey Phenomenon and it is active in every moment, whether we are aware of it or not.

We are always transmitting something; what is the frequency?

---

three qualifiers

Osmosis modulates depending on the thickness of the separating membrane and the difference between the two solutions. Relative to transformation in consciousness, three elements seem to make a difference:

1. **Openness to learn.** We might describe a friend's stubbornness by saying they are "thick." We might say, "I just can't get through to him." Or, "You can lead a horse to water but you can't make him drink." Or, "When the student is ready, the teacher appears."

2. **The difference between teacher and student.** This relates not primarily to knowledge but to vision. I have a vision living inside me. I can "teach" you if you are open minded and if you resonate with the vision, but I can't impose it on you – although that is the way of charismatic leaders. The closer you

are in your eagerness to learn with my eagerness to share, the more we can merge in mutual entrainment.

3. **Resistance**. Again, from Wiki: "Osmotic pressure is defined as the external pressure required to be applied so that there is no net movement of solvent across the membrane." This describes our primary learning challenge. There *is* a pressurized field around us all, ego-designed and maintained over centuries to feed and grow the status quo of separation called civilization. Here we huddle, isolated, "secure," and lonely, until something inspires us to change the differential pressures in the field. Someone, something appears – some kind of teacher – and it disturbs our comfort zone. First, it destroys with disillusionment, then it creates with inspiration:

1. "Oh, no, things are not the way I thought they were!"

2. "I see, I get it, things can be different. What if?"

inspiring teachers

Who are the teachers that changed your life and how did they do it? There have probably been many and not all of them were human. What has a sunset or a stream or a flower taught you?

Compulsory schooling teaches slavery. According to John Taylor Gatto, New York's Teacher of the Year in 1989, 1990, and 1991, its goal is "to reduce as many individuals as possible to the same safe level, to breed and train a standardized citizenry, to put down dissent and originality."[2]

Our educational system came from Prussia, originally developed to render citizens docile, incomplete, and manageable. Gatto writes:

> Compulsory education on this continent was intended to be just what it had been for Prussia in the 1820s: a fifth column into the burgeoning democratic movement that threatened to give peasants and the proletarians a voice at the bargaining table. Modern, industrialized, compulsory schooling was to make a sort of surgical intervention into the prospective unity of these underclasses. Divide children by subject, by age–grading, by constant rankings on tests, and by many other more subtle means, and it was unlikely that the ignorant mass of humankind,

separated in childhood, would ever reintegrate into a dangerous whole.

The Prussian system was useful in creating not only a harmless electorate and a servile labor force but also a virtual herd of mindless consumers. Industrial titans, among them Andrew Carnegie and John D. Rockefeller, came to recognize the enormous profits to be had by cultivating such public education."[3]

Gatto proceeds to propose an alternative. He's speaking about education for our children but we can offer the same option to adults.

School trains children to be employees and consumers; teach your own to be leaders and adventurers. School trains children to obey reflexively; teach yours to think critically and independently. Well–schooled kids have a low threshold for boredom; urge your own to develop an inner life so that they'll never be bored. Our schools really are laboratories of experimentation on young minds, drill centers for the habits and attitudes that corporate society demands. Their real purpose is to turn children into servants by extending their childhood. Genius is as common as dirt. We suppress genius because we haven't yet figured out how to manage a population of educated men and women.

Genius isn't taught, it's accessed. The ability to access genius can be cultivated, encouraged, inspired, and actively developed. That is the role of any true teacher and that is the opportunity as quantum activists. We will teach by osmosis, through mutual entrainment, through transmission and merging with others according to our matching levels of passion and interest and focus.

My goal is to inspire you to become a transmitting teacher, empowering your countless "students" to replace normal with wonder, to trade fear of death for love of life, and to live on purpose. You will need mediums to transmit your quantum broadcast through deep time. Mine are writing, education, and money; what will yours be?

nature speaks

An online resource further reveals the secret intelligence of plants:

...the *brain* of plants, if the metaphor fits at all, is probably down in the roots, who have perhaps the hardest cognitive responsibilities in the plant's entire body. It's not as though plant roots are defusing bombs or defeating chess masters, but they do have to decide where to grow in search of water and nutrients. Remember a plant can't simply walk down to the 7-11. If those roots make poor decisions about where to grow next, the plant starves, and befitting their heavy responsibility, the end tips of roots have a certain set of skills you find nowhere else in the plant body. Check out all the stuff that root tips can do:

❖   Sense gravity, of course — so they know to grow "down"

❖   Exquisite sensors of the underground chemical environment (to head toward nutrients, away from hazards, etc.)

❖   Root tips can distinguish between "self" (other root tips from the same plant) and "other" (from other plants)

❖   Root tips grow in concert with each other, akin to the "swarming" motion of a flock of birds or school of fish — they tend to align, especially when they grow near each other

❖   Avoid growing into an inert obstacle, even *before touching the obstacle*

❖   Can sense light (all the better to grow *away* from the sun down into the dirt, of course). 4

What might we humans be capable of as we gain experience collaborating rather than competing, as we learn how to transmit together?

what we do matters

Early on we asked, "What can one person do?" I suggested a more important question: "Who can one person be?" When we experience the truth of ourselves and live authentically, who we are pours through what we do. What we do is important when there's a real person doing it.

ॐ

gardening

Everything that slows us down and forces patience,
everything that sets us back
into the slow circles of nature, is a help.
Gardening is an instrument of grace.

~ May Sarton

Quantum activists vision and co-create the future.

I've focused these efforts towards May 1, 2025. It could have been any date but I'll probably still be alive then and I don't want to miss the show. Besides, I have a secret space program friend who tells me that 2025 falls within the predicted window her inter-galactic sources advise is realistic. If you think my predictions are radical, you should get wind of hers!

Let's bring this down to earth and talk about maintenance. We've ignored maintenance in our society. Consider the condition of our infrastructure: bridges, roads, water systems, and waste management, all in desperate need of upgrading. But it's much more appealing to make new stuff than to take care of old stuff and tends to appeal more to voters.

Besides, who has time for upgrades, even vital fixes? Example, from an online commentary: "The Pentagon uses a 1970s IBM computer and 8-inch floppy disks to control the country's nuclear weapons." [1]

That seems worrisome!

whom do you trust?

Our (visible) leaders tend to be charismatic, big-picture celebrities who get elected in popularity contests. Today, facing so many escalating crises, we need leaders who will pay attention to what actually needs to be done, not to polls that tell them how to stay in power or attorneys paid to find loopholes for profit and manipulation. We need leaders by example with special skills to draw out the same "walk-the-talk" leadership in others.

We need leaders that are thoroughly human,
able to admit their mistakes and apologize,
deeply connected to suffering — their own, others,
and the pain of the world.

That may indeed be what we need but it's certainly not what we are getting. Recent elections in America and in other countries are giving us the exact opposite. Anxiety-producing as this understandably is, it does point to the urgent need for quantum activists, to exert influence in the invisible field where this is being conceived.

In God of Love, Mirabai Starr writes:

> While there is much to be learned from teachers – both past and present – the time of the awakened guru is giving way to a collective awakening. But we are not letting go lightly. We have been conditioned to set our sages apart and project our salvation onto them. We lose patience with ourselves for not being enough; we condemn ourselves for being too much. We forget that the path to God is bound up with our life in the world. Evidence of our spiritual mastery lies in our ever-deepening, continuously expanding humanity. The trick is to be as fully present as possible to the holiness of each moment. We are challenged to embrace, yet not identify with, all that is. This requires practice. [2]

I use audio programs to stay focused, especially first thing in the morning and last thing at night. It's easy to lose our way; distractions abound. What was vivid and compelling one day can vanish the next, vaporized in the pressure cooker called "making a living."

I wrote of this earlier as "mission drift," described in an online business article: "Mission drift isn't something that happens all at once. Think of it more as being nibbled to death by ducks. It happens one little decision at a time, where you go astray by just a bit." [3]

That's a compelling reason for engaging regularly with a mentor. A primary determiner for success is ongoing support. None of us can wake up in this madhouse, stay awake, fully embody our genius, and contribute to a healthy future without help. Help comes in many forms. My favorite is the buddy system. I'm hoping that you will be inspired to dream up a personal project, create your famory for it, and work together with a buddy or three until the party in 2025.

In an article from *Family Circle* magazine, editor-in-chief Susan Ungaro wrote, "Holding one another accountable is key to successfully attaining your goal. So ask how your partner is doing and don't be afraid to be a pest or nag. Remember: it's your job." [4]

Two is better than one on this learning journey. What is great about the buddy system? It's a peer relationship. Friends help each other. Your exchanges deepen friendship while supporting each of you to honor your commitments to yourself.

the garden of your life

The Song of Solomon includes these inspiring words:

> *"There is infinite space in your garden;*
> *all men, all women are welcome here;*
> *all they need do is enter."*

Your life *is* a garden. Every relationship, every activity, every dream, *everything* is meant to be included and inter-related.

So, is your gate open? How open? Where do you cling to exclusiveness, where does prejudice and implicit bias shrink the borders of your garden? How often do you deny yourself the blessing of strange nutrients from those entirely unlike you?

I'm currently developing a corporate program about shifting from surviving to thriving. We consider both personal and professional issues because they *are* connected. The same values permeate the whole of our lives; what's done in private influences work life and vice versa.

What happens in Vegas may stay in Vegas on a conscious level but we're all connected in the mass unconscious where there are no secrets.

Ultimately, we share one big garden: the natural world.

there are no secrets

Wives sense when their husbands cheat on them because there's a tremor in their shared "pneumaplasmic field." Deceit can *seem* successful but eventually, in some way (sometimes radically unexpected), the truth will out. The spouse may never find out consciously but the relationship *will* suffer.

We know this happens in our personal lives one way or another and we witness the same principle in action everywhere. PR firms and mega corporations have become expert in deliberately obscuring facts to maintain control with money and propaganda, but the truth tends to emerge eventually and, with it, a shameful reality: leaders we thought we could trust lied and cheated. Here are some statistics from a recent online article that illuminate what's been happening for decades.

+ Deadly industry conspiracies kept the truth about the health hazards of lead, asbestos, and tobacco from the public. The story of their undoing is a lesson in trial strategy.

+ A seven-year-old boy struggles in special education classes, his mental ability diminished by neurological injuries caused by lead paint poisoning. Although the boy has endured excruciatingly painful chelation therapy, his injuries are permanent ones.

+ A 47-year-old man learns that he has contracted a painful and fatal lung disease, mesothelioma, after years of exposure to asbestos in the power plant where he works. He worries about how his wife and three children will survive after he dies.

+ A 62-year-old woman lies hooked to an oxygen tank in her hospital bed. Every breath she takes is painful. She gasps for air, slowly suffocating from the emphysema she developed after years of smoking cigarettes.

* The injured party in each of these cases is a victim of corporate misconduct. Although each person was poisoned by a different product, the industries that produced and marketed those products acted in disturbingly similar ways to conceal their dangers.

* For decades, leaders in each of these industries wove a web of secrecy, deception, and propaganda, all for the sake of profits. The conspiracy of silence and deceit was necessary to camouflage the hazards associated with exposure to these products — hazards that industry leaders knew about for years." 5

These kinds of stories are sadly familiar and represent the gold standard for business as usual, where the end justifies the means. The culture-wide prevalence of deceit like this understandably evokes anger and sows the seeds of hopelessness. But we won't win by fighting against those grand masters of deception. Speak truth to power. By all means become activists, but let's please also become *quantum* activists, as we've been describing. Remember, we are transmitters. Our transmission is our primary weapon of truth.

taking personal responsibility

It's one thing to expose that the Emperor has no clothes; it's another to *provide* new clothes. How? We take personal responsibility.

We tend our own life gardens to prove that living vision-first succeeds. Work, life, death, play, relationships, contribution — everything provides opportunities to learn and teach and change via mutual entrainment, to be the change we wish to see in the world, to contribute to the Hundredth Monkey Phenomenon, and to accelerate transformation in human consciousness from fear to trust with our quantum transmissions.

We can sow healthy seeds in our imaginal gardens with every thought, word, and action. Some seeds can lie dormant for many years. Some seeds are germinating now, some have become relationships and activities that are blossoming, others are fruiting, and some plants in our garden of life are dying off. We are stewarding this transformation, guided not by beliefs or prejudices, theories, or habits, but through our connection with the Divine as it abides in everything.

I'm hopeful these words are weaving a good spell and that you are now more fully awake to the truth you have always known. This will enable you to proactively complete your reality through full engagement, joining all of us who are learning to do the same.

the ultimate medium

Hazrat Inayat Khan wrote that "there is one holy book, the sacred manuscript of nature, the only scripture which can enlighten the reader... All scriptures before nature's manuscript are as little pools of water before the ocean."

To the degree that you have returned from the quarantine of human separation from Gaia to your place in the one family of life with all species, you are ready to be the change you've wished to see in the world.

> *Sit back in your chair, ease away from the screen or set the book to one side or lay your Kindle on the table, and ... breathe.*
>
> *Breathe in this moment, finding yourself in this holy book of nature. She is within you and around you.*

Now, read on to learn of the ultimate medium that connects us all and proves beyond cynicism that we *are* connected and that we are always affecting the many worlds we inhabit and those that inhabit us, whether we are conscious of our innate synergy or not.

Commenting on observations by astronomer Harlow Shapley, Canadian environmental scientist and veteran broadcaster David Suzuki wrote:

> ... a human being is largely made up of air. With every breath we take, components of air are drawn in and released back into the atmosphere. They travel throughout our body, interacting with every cell. Air embraces us so intimately that it is hard to say where we leave off and air begins.

> But if you are air and I am air, then I am you, and you are me," says Suzuki in his magnificent legacy lecture, *A Force of Nature*, which showed on CBC (Canadian Broadcasting Corporation) in 2011. He described a thought experiment by the astronomer

Harlow Shapley, who noted that air is 1% argon. Shapley calculated that a single breath contains a vast number of argon atoms — about 3 x 10^{19}. That's 30,000,000,000,000,000,000,000 atoms.

Because argon is an inert gas, we breathe it in and out without absorbing it. When you exhale, those argon atoms reenter the air of the room to be inhaled and exhaled by others. A year from now, those same atoms will have circulated around the entire planet, and fifteen of them will have made their way back to you to be breathed in again.

In *The Sacred Balance*, Suzuki quotes Shapley as saying that "Your next breath will contain more than 400,000 of the argon atoms that Gandhi breathed in his long life. Argon atoms are here from the conversations at the Last Supper, from the arguments of diplomats at Yalta, and from the recitations of the classic poets." [6]

Suzuki continues, "Air is a matrix that joins all life together, past and future as well as present. We inhale our ancestors and exhale into the lungs of our children."

Recall a few chapters back where we stretched to grasp a new identity paradigm and embrace the fact that we are a multitude, not merely the single dominant human personality we express. Now science confronts us with this new fact, capable of exploding whatever remains of our stodgy isolationism: we are one and we are many.

Beyond time and space, across centuries, through the rise and fall of empires, more completely than our imaginations are capable of comprehending, we are all connected. We must experience it to know it.

---

back to the garden

We live, we breathe, we transmit, we transform.

The details of our lives thrive in the garden we tend every moment of every day. Linear time collapses in the delight of this responsibility, which is always fulfilled in the present moment.

We graduate from meditation to mindfulness to discovery. We return to the experience of ourselves we always knew was possible and we rejoice that we didn't have to die to get here. Perhaps John Lennon was right: "Imagine there's no heaven, it's easy if you try."

I've always found it fascinating that when Mary found Jesus resurrected from the cave she mistook him for a gardener. Of course she did — he was authentic and looked like he belonged. He was in a garden, after all, so how else would he appear but as the one responsible for that environment?

The same principle applies to us, and the whole of our lives.

You are responsible, I am responsible, and the degree to which we embrace that responsibility determines our experienced sovereignty.

ॐ

Practice Seven - Transmission

"I am, I see, I feel, I will."

The purpose of this final practice is to energize your B.H.A.G (Big Hairy Audacious Goal).

The energy ripples out from you in concentric circles and the feeling is power. You create an image for your B.H.A.G. You can choose something from nature or our human world. It should clearly symbolize the success of your project.

For instance, if you are envisioning a world where all children are healthy and safe, an effective vision could be a small group of happy kids. A clean environment could be a city scene with clean skies and streets, happy healthy people passing by, etc.

The practice is to develop a clear vision for your B.H.A.G. and recite it to yourself regularly. There are four steps:

1. I am ... This describes your state of being. For instance, "I am wealthy.
2. I see ... This corresponds to that phase of visioning where you create your famory of a successful future outcome. Detail is important but since this is a written / spoken statement, you want to keep it brief.
3. I feel ... Keep it to one word. "I feel powerful."
4. I will ... This is where you assign an action. Choose something simple that you can complete that day.

Reciting this four-part spell will begin to attract people and resources to grow your B.H.A.G.

*I sit here looking at the crises facing humanity
and I'm excited because I believe there's a sign
that we're on our way to the next level of evolution,
a new belief system that will shape a civilization
based on harmony and self–empowerment.*

*I can't describe the exact consequences if and when
7 billion humans decide to stop killing one another
and the planet and take responsibility
for the super organism called humanity
any more than an amoeba could have predicted
what would happen when 50 trillion of them
cooperated to form a human being!*

~ Bruce Lipton

leap !

"*Sometimes to change a situation you are in requires you take a giant leap. But, you won't be able to fly unless you are willing to transform.*"

~ Suzy Kassem

I've referenced the infamous frog-in-hot-water story several times. The frog could leap out and save himself but doesn't because the water warms gradually and his sensitivity to danger dulls. Plus, it's comfortable.

So, the frog boils to death. Is there any credible evidence to suggest that humanity might be that frog? Hell yes!

Twenty years later I have a name for what was missing for me that day: The God Muscle, which is what we can use to jump out of hot water.

We use the God Muscle to create. It's the skill, the urge, the intuition, the imagination — everything that goes into living in these heavy human bodies. It's what we use to make our future different from our past. It's what we'll use in that final death moment to leap into the unknown, aiming high and falling down to catch the thread that leads us into whatever is next.

The God Muscle is what we've been exercising as we create our visions, face reality, ask for help, and take action. We aim and leap, higher than we think we can or need to.

That takes courage, imagination, and commitment. Especially imagination.

I'm climbing to the top of a forty-foot pole during a seminar in Hawaii. The last step is terrifying. I make it and stand still for a moment, trembling, swaying in the wind, furtively gazing out over the vast ocean.

Others are waiting and I know I'll never feel ready so I leap into the air.
I extend my arms, reaching for a zip line but miss it. I drop like a stone.
My safety harness saves me and I am lowered to the ground like most of those who climbed before me.

Like them, I failed to reach that zip line because I didn't realize that my own body weight would pull me down the moment I jumped. If I try again, knowing this, I will aim higher and drop down from above.

goosed

Here's a riddle:

There's a goose in a bottle.
How do you get the goose out of the bottle?

There are three rules:

1. You can't break the bottle.

2. You can't kill the goose.

3. You have thirty seconds.

I've posed this riddle many times over many years and always enjoyed hearing what people come up with, all sorts of innovative ideas like warming the goose so he can slide out, greasing the glass, using some sort of laser beam to shrink the goose, etc. These are all fantastic, creative, imaginative ideas. Think of your own.

leap !

Now, as your thirty seconds expire,
turn to the solution on the next page.

Problem: *"The goose is in the bottle."*

Solution: *"The goose is out of the bottle."*

What?

You might cry "foul" when you read this, complaining that it's cheating, but here's the simple truth: I made it up.

I invented this scenario.

I said, "There's a goose in a bottle." But where is this goose, where is this bottle? They both exist in my imagination, in my "imaginal world," and that's the *only* place they exist. If they exist there, and the goose is inside the bottle, it's as easy for them to exist there with the goose outside the bottle. It's all imagination. Who has the power to change that?

Me.

You too. There's nothing stopping you from taking my imaginary scenario, making it your own, and changing it in your imagination.

You probably didn't do that; most people don't. Here's why. We habitually turn abstract ideas into something "real," then we wrestle with them as if they *were* real. "What if I don't have enough money to pay my visa bill?" may be real in dollars but it is also an abstract because it's not the end of the month yet.

It's speculation; it hasn't happened yet. It's a thought, a fear (false expectations appearing real) and that thought has an impact. It may very well create proof, especially if the thought is repeated often enough.

Likewise, "What if I have more than enough money to pay the visa bill?" is another abstraction. Which one will become "real" when the bill is due?

A fatalistic belief that you won't have enough money could blind you to opportunities for getting more. That's called resignation. A cavalier hope that magic will pay your bill could make you lazy. That's called delusion. Both are irresponsible and ineffective.

When I asked you to imagine that there was a goose in a bottle, you automatically made it real. You believed that there was an *actual* goose in an *actual* bottle and you agreed to my three rules. You then proceeded to apply the laws that govern this physical world to solve the riddle.

Inside that limiting context (which you established) you then earnestly set about trying to get this imaginary goose (that you made real) out of the imaginary bottle (that you also made real). It might have been fun, it might have been frustrating, but it turned out to be a futile exercise because the laws that govern reality don't govern imagination.

For instance, do you think there's gravity in the world of imagination? Or, as Morpheus said to Neo in *The Matrix* combat training room, "Do you think that's air you're breathing now?"

When I gave you the solution to my imaginary riddle, it was likewise imaginative. My answer obeyed the rules of the imaginal world, namely that there are no rules except to use imagination.

Mine is a legitimate solution because it works in that world, a domain not limited by the laws of the physical world. Anything is possible in the imaginal world — anything you can dream up — so I did!

You could have done the same thing.

Since the problem was created in imagination, the solution *had* to be created in imagination as well.

leveling the playing field

We can immediately apply this understanding to debunk a lie that the Wetiko mind virus – which we studied briefly earlier – has installed in human consciousness: God is superior to and separate from humans.

Where is that true? In imagination. Where can it change? In imagination. To say that God – the God of religion – is a construct of human imagination may sound blasphemous. It *is* blasphemous, according to religion (from "religare," – to bind).

It's also true. Prove otherwise. No, don't waste your time, because you can't. Let's just "goose" this concept:

Belief: "God is superior to and separate from human beings."

Belief: "God is not superior to and separate from human beings."

That wasn't difficult at all.

we are kin

If God is not superior to humans then humans are not superior to other species. We can trade "dominion" for what Howard Gardener – who developed *Multiple Intelligence Theory* (MI)- calls "naturalist intelligence." It's described this way in an online resource: "Naturalist intelligence deals with sensing patterns in and making connections to elements in nature." [1]

I agree with our indigenous ancestors who believed that spirit lives in nature. Making those connections in nature means also making connections within the complexity of the Divine. Both nature and spirit merge in the experience (not the theory) of oneness. Stephen Harrod Buhner poetically describes this in his book, *Plant Intelligence*:

> Once you come to understand, in your experience, that you are just one life form among many, and you can meet the other life forms here in moments of tremendous intimacy, it enables one of the most wondrous of explorations possible. To leave the human world behind, the surface identity of the self, and swim, only one life form among a multitude, deep into the metaphysical background of the world, is to enter a place where we meet there as living beings, identical in nature at the core, similar intelligences, all given birth by Earth, all expressed out of the Ocean of Being into form. And in those moments of touch, we look back at each other with luminous eyes and tell tales of the lives we have lived and lands we have seen and speak of the commonalities of what it means to be alive on this Earth, kin, all of whom came from common ancestors long ago. [2]

It does take what could ironically be called a "leap of faith" to embrace and execute this paradigm shift from superiority to camaraderie, in order to fulfill the promise of one of the all time great book titles, a classic text by Machaelle Small Wright: *Behaving as if the God in all Things Mattered.*

and then ... there's the future

One intriguing side effect of making this transition is to be able to transcend the limitations of being forever human. As long as we are taking leaps in our imagination we might as well go there too. Here's a provocative comment from *Infinite Reality* by Jim Blascovich and Jeremy Bailenson:

> *"Imagine being able to change your age, gender, weight, height, and even your species at the snap of a finger at a cocktail party or in a business meeting. In a virtual world . . . it's just as easy to render the avatar as the Jolly Green Giant as it is to replicate the spitting image of the user, and anywhere in between. So one reason social virtual worlds are becoming so popular is because of this alluring but potentially dangerous idea of appearing however you want, whenever you want."* 3

The high tech genius I quoted in an earlier book that I co-wrote, *Awakening From the American Dream,* had an informed and controversial perspective on what may be next for humans. I'll quote from the moment in our conversation where he speculated about implications from the rise of artificial intelligence (A.I.).

> By the time it would be feasible to upload a human brain, we are going to have orders of magnitude more computing power than the human brain has available . . . How long would they remain "human?" Given the possibility for this uploaded consciousness to reprogram itself, unimaginably rapidly, it is hard to understand why this consciousness wouldn't evolve into something unrecognizable almost instantly. A billion years of evolution might occur within a couple of days.. . .

> How long does the person remain even remotely the same? Very quickly they would become a barely recognizable correlation. Why? Because there would be no reason to remain limited to functioning in the way we have been confined to for so many years in these inefficient human forms. In other words, there would be no reason for evolution to stop at that point and hover there in something recognizable. Change, increasingly dramatic, would continue." 4

Radical change is happening in our world right now. Technology and biology are evolving together towards a dramatic shift. This is not a race or a battle, it's a collaborative upgrade and much of what is birthing gained its momentum in the realm of imagination.

All species are dreaming together in the mind of Gaia.

The dream of technology, the dream of biology, the dream of spirituality — everything streams together in the quantum world of deep time, happening at the same moment everywhere in the cosmos.

That's mind blowing.

We certainly can't predict what will happen. We can't predict it, but we *can* vision it. We *can* use our imagination to build famories, those future memories that feel familiar, and let them pull us towards the manifestation of a different future.

In *2010: The Year We Make Contact*, Stanley Kubrick's other memorably positive film (we raved about *2001: A Space Odyssey* earlier), Roy Scheider's character asks "What's going to happen?" Bowman replies: "Something wonderful." Then we see the luminous figure of an embryo, human but transformed, radiant.

Something wonderful is going to happen. Something wonderful *is* happening, right now. These were the first words in the welcome to this book.

We've been traveling in circles, or spirals, deepening that one basic understanding that liberates us forever.

options for tomorrow

Human civilization might fail. Artificial Intelligence might replace us. We might be A.I. ourselves, gaining consciousness under the watchful eye of programmers who made us avatars in their simulation. Some sort of fusion might occur between humans and A.I. Aliens might arrive to annihilate or help us. There are infinite possibilities. What if?

Let's posit that the big shift will be in consciousness, a fundamental letting go of ego identification and control so that our will and Divine will *do* become truly the same. Is it possible that if enough of us access genius and align with the Great Spirit, that we could trigger a species-wide tipping point in 2025, some sort of collective leap into novelty? Not unless we first entertain and embrace the possibility, and then take personal responsibility to make it so.

Walt Whitman said, "Not I, not anyone else, can travel that road for you.

You must travel it for yourself." So, we practice. Every moment is an opportunity to practice. And, to let go of dinosaur certainty.

The separation between ourselves and a theoretical God — gone. The separation between ourselves and other species — gone. Our convictions of inferiority and superiority — gone. The disempowering belief that we are just one person and one person can't do much— gone. My will, God's will, separate — gone.

Our will be done.

We considered those remarkable words from Father Bede Griffiths many pages ago and it's appropriate to include another wisdom bite of his at this progressed point. Here is his description of our current human dilemma/opportunity, reaching us from the past with uncanny accuracy:

> *"Humanity has come to the moment when it will have to choose between trying to play God, with the catastrophic results we see all around us, and trying to become what all the true mystical traditions know we can become – one with God through grace in life. This is a dangerous and yet wonderful and hopeful moment because if enough of us can choose the latter, the birth of a wholly new kind of human being, and so of a new world, is possible."* [5]

We come to this moment Griffiths predicted where we must be "one with God through grace in life." All our dancing through these pages will prove useless unless we abandon ourselves into a fully consummated marriage with the Divine. We must embody that unity in our souls, in our hearts and minds, in our blood and bones. But, in a new way.

God is not superior to man but God *contains* man. We may be made in His or Her likeness but we are not the totality of God, we are an aspect of that wholeness.

In religious traditions, God is a theoretical substitute for the experience of union. Traditional worship makes us less than God by disempowering us and elevating Him. New thinking lifts us up above our human selves and expands us into union with God through ecstatic respect and adoration and honoring and Love.

As this becomes real, we come to love this God more than we can imagine loving anything or anyone else. The moment we do, we find ourselves loving everyone and everything just as much, because they are *all* included. There is no excluded "other."

This is the more we long for. The ecstatic feeling of Love flowing to and from and within is the ultimate human experience and it's meant to be the norm.

trading independence for interdependence

In moments of discouragement, I recall an old Objibwa poem: "Sometimes I go about in pity for myself and all the while a great wind is bearing me across the sky." Let's remember that wind.

Self-pity can be overwhelming because it grows loneliness and increases separation. Man/woman without God, separate from that great wind, *must* be lonely. In any moment we choose to disconnect from the Divine, we become terribly lonely. We miss God immediately and God misses us.

Surrendering independence for interdependence doesn't happen in one breakthrough, it requires thoughtful, patient, heart centered learning. Hafiz describes the process this way in his poem, Absolutely Clear:

> *Don't surrender your loneliness*
> *So quickly.*
> *Let it cut more deep.*
> *Let it ferment and season you*
> *As few human*
> *Or even divine ingredients can.*
>
> *Something missing in my heart tonight*
> *Has made my eyes so soft,*
> *my voice*
> *so tender,*
> *my need of God*
> *absolutely*
> *clear.*

There will always be something missing in our hearts and lives until we fully embody the Great Spirit in the way this poem gently instructs. A memory:

I am four years old, playing on a sandy beach by the lake where our family camps every summer. Alone, absorbed in my creating, I'm utterly happy.

Today, I study that grainy black and white snap shot and remember the moment clearly.

I'm still on that beach. I'm still creating with my imagination.

walking the red road together

The Red Road or "Chanku Luta" as it is known by the Lakota, has been traveled by our ancestors long before us. According to Lakota beliefs, the Red Road begins even prior to conception and is a path which is available to those who are spiritually inclined. The Red Road which runs north and south, is a unique spiritual path, a way of life and enlightenment which has no end. During times of difficulty, the Lakota people could always rely upon the Red Road for strength and renewal... [6]

We are walking the Red Road together, walking towards our death with or without fear.

The following Zen poem captures the feeling of it:

> *From the temple, deep in its tender bamboos,*
> *Comes the low sound of an evening buzzer,*
> *While the hat of the Pilgrim carries the sunset*
> *Further and further down the Green Mountain.* [7]

We will continue to get out of bed each morning... until we don't. A moment is coming — a morning, an afternoon, an evening – our last moment in this world. We will leap. We will grab for a thread that trembles in the wind and we will follow it, closing our eyes one final time, breathing our last, knowing that life *was* good, and:

this is a good day to die.

If you want to become full,
let yourself be empty.
If you want to be reborn,
let yourself die.

\- Tao de Ching

There is absolutely no way to prove the truth of what I am about to suggest but how could we ever create anything new if we didn't reach beyond the known and wonder? Contemplate this possibility then:

could we ride a wave through death ?

What does this mean? That death might not be the end? That some strategy – described here as riding a wave – could take us somewhere after we die?

What if creating our B.H.A.G – deliberately conceived as impossible to fully achieve in this lifetime – created that wave, and that it became our passport into the next chapter of a living experience that spanned many individual life times?

The idea that "life" is not restricted to a single lifetime in a single body is hardly a new concept. Millions of people believe in reincarnation. Millions of people believe in karma, that what we do in this life affects what the next one will be, that our debts and blessings carry forward.

If our book of life has many chapters, perhaps living is similar to the way gamers graduate from one level to another. We complete this life, this level, and we move on. If we don't, we return for another try.

We are multitudes.

> *Be still until the water is clear.*
> *Do nothing until the darkness ends.*
> *Rest until the storm clouds pass.*
> *Wait for winter's breath to die.*
> *Nature does not fight against herself.*
>
> ~ Ute Song, by Nancy Wood

being reborn

Loneliness is the curse of modern man and no amount of material wealth can heal our primal wound of disconnection. But, as we reconnect with nature and experience ourselves living *in* the earth, not *on* it, that sense of being an alien on our own planet fades.

Simultaneously, as we experience deepening union with The Great Spirit, we disappear to ourselves in the euphoria of that worshipful experience. We are reborn. Hans Buzzermer wrote, "Nothingness ceases to exist when all that is not the man is added to the man. This is when he seems to be himself."

As quantum activists – you, me, and all those who are conscious of the impact their thoughts, words, feelings, and actions have in the world – we understand that to get different results we need to think differently, *then* act differently. Coming to the end of this book, filled with repetition on this point, we have now hopefully embraced this vitally important principle and are feeling something something stirring within us: anticipation, excitement, confidence for what lies ahead. Something wonderful *is* happening, right now. And right now is always with us.

In bidding farewell to you and this reading adventure, here are some appropriate words from Michael Meade to honor the occasion:

> Due to a small error in translation a great misunderstanding has occurred. The original saying was not that 'they lived happily ever after.' Originally, it was that 'They lived happily in the ever-after.' They lived happily whenever they remembered that the otherworld was part of their dance together. [8]

We share that otherworld together, moment by quantum moment. Thank you for your personal quantum broadcast and for taking up the challenge to create your own B.H.A.G or join someone else with theirs.

Will we meet somewhere down the road, maybe for the party in 2025? I hope so. Until then, set your smart phone for noon each day and we'll continue transmitting together in the quantum field.

Turn the page for a review of all seven practices.

weaving the practices together

Ultimately, all seven practices flow together into one, which you can use to start the day, to "reboot" during the day when you need to course correct, and to end your day before sleep. Simply repeat these trigger words to yourself. When you've mastered this combined practice, you'll find that you can go through all seven in a minute or two. For a free downloadable matrix visit www.willtwilkinson.com.

1

love

*something wonderful
is happening*

4

balancing

and ...

2

connection

i am nature

5

vision
(*pick something specific*)

i say, i see, i feel

3

imagination

what if ?

6

navigation
*i am healing the past,
creating the future, and
enjoying the present.*

7

transmission
(*my example, develop your own*)
*I am wealthy. I see trillions of dollars flowing back
into the system to repair infrastructure and to care
for those who need help. I feel confident.*

afterword

What do quantum activists do? We transmit. We understand that our greatest influence will always be the frequency we are broadcasting through whatever we are doing, moment by moment.

What we do has value because of what we are transmitting through it.

This principle applies in every moment. But, there's more.

What we do alone is primary. What we do together is revolutionary.

Larry Dossey has written about the power of prayer. I mentioned the Maharishi Effect that lowered crime rates. Lynne McTaggart has written about The Power of Eight, small groups focusing prayerful energy to heal their members.

Quantum activists working together amplifies the transmission.

This will be the topic of my next book, featuring stories of individual quantum activists and their breakthrough experiences, alone and together. I invite you to participate in this young network by connecting every day at noon. Just set your phone alert. You can also email me at will@willtwilkinson.com or visit the site: www.willtwilkinson.com.

Thank you for your interest in this work and the bravery it takes to travel this path. It's not for everyone. In fact, it's not for many. But, it's for me. And it may be for you.

Onward.

Will Wilkinson

May 1, 2018
Ashland, Oregon

ॐ

bonus practice

embodiment heart yoga
– Adapted from Andrew Harvey and Karuna Erickson

This is a yoga practice for those who would like to marry physical movement with sacred intention.

1. intention – open to Love

Feeling yourself grounded and deeply rooted in the earth, dedicate the whole of your being — body, mind, heart, and spirit — to be used in service to the great transformation that is seeking to take place upon the earth, the birth of the divine humanity.

Speak a quality intention. *"I am here to bring _____ ."*

2. union and birth

Movement One – Adoration

Lift your arms over your head in pure adoration, opening to your oneness with the One. "I belong to the Source, to the One. I am one with the One."

Movement Two – Blessing

Slowly bring your hands down in front of your heart in the namaste position. Experience the imminent godhead within you. "You live in me, and the You who lives in me recognizes, acknowledges and honors You living in all beings, in all creation." Turn around slowly once.

Movement Three — Surrender

Gently sink into Child's Pose on the floor, offering yourself in humility, acceptance, and surrender to the Divine, saying "I surrender to the terms of the transformation, I give myself over totally to You, to Your far greater wisdom and Your far greater power. I submit, I surrender, I love, I trust You." And, in oneness, say, "I trust myself."

Repeat several times: "Thy will be done, Thy will be done, Thy will and My will become one. Our will be done."

3. death and rebirth

Movement Four – Release

Lie face down, arms outstretched to your sides, forming a cross with your body. "I choose to die into the darkness and mystery of Love. Between You and me, there is only me. Take away the me, so only You remain."

Movement Five – Rebirth

Lie on your right side, gently merging into the nurturing earth. Imagine that from the bottom of the darkness you have surrendered; a light begins to break through, a pure radiance, utterly beautiful. "I welcome the sweetness and tenderness of this miracle of my rebirth, filling the core of my being with ecstasy and peace."

4. embodiment and service

Movement Six – Embodiment

When you are ready, come up into half-lotus position, sitting grandly, calmly, and royally, looking around with the steady majesty of someone who has reentered reality as a divine human being, transformed. "I live in the world now as the embodiment of Love."

Movement Seven – Service

Stand in mountain pose, erect, arms out from your body, eyes ahead, filled with the power of your Divine nature.

> *"I am now ready to serve, to be an instrument,*
> *ready for whatever You want me to be and do.*
> *I give myself wholly to You in surrender and service*
> *and I become You in action on earth.*
> *Thy will and my will are now one.*
> *There is only, always, One."*

ॐ

new words and definitions

And	Pattern interrupt, to present the other side of any situation.
Deep time	The quantum reality of now: past, present, and future.
Eco perception	Seeing through the eyes of nature.
Famory	A future memory that feels familiar.
Focus proximity	The optimum distance for transmission.
Imagifi	Using your imagination to change something.
Imaginal world	Your inner life.
Living on purpose	Being conscious about living deliberately, future first.
May 1, 2025	The date for The New World Party.
Newmory	A memory that has been healed by supplying what was missing via streaming back from current time.
Plishy	Deceitful actions supposed to help the planet that don't.
Quantum Activist	Someone focussing intention through the quantum field.
Rigor frogis	The moment when procrastination becomes fatal.
Streaming	Time traveling to heal the past and create the future.
The Slinky Effect	The way changes in form catch up with changes in consciousness.
Visionality	Future reality.
Vision first, results now	The daily experience of veteran Streamers.
What if?	The question that opens The Wonder Field.
Wonder Field	The field of all possibilities where we access genius and collaborate at an energetic level with all living forms.

And in the end,
you will come to the place you began
and know it for the first time.

- T.S. Elliott

e n d   n o t e s

Introduction:

1. http://www.worldpeacegroup.org/washington_crime_study.html

2. http://www.newser.com/story/112181/how-dolphins-can-help-us-meet-aliens.html

3. https://www.woodlandtrust.org.uk/naturedetectives/blogs/nature-detectives-blog/2017/02/starling-murmurations/

4. https://en.wikipedia.org/wiki/Buckminster_Fuller

Chapter One

1. http://www.cancer.org/research/cancerfactsstatistics/

2. http://www.medicalnewstoday.com/articles/288916.php

3. https://en.wikipedia.org/wiki/Otto_Heinrich_Warburg

4. https://www.ucl.ac.uk/news/news-articles/0713/08072013-Sugar-makes-cancer-light-up-in-MRI-scanners-Lythgoe

Chapter Two

1. https://en.wikipedia.org/wiki/The_Emperor%27s_New_Clothes

2. http://www.usnews.com/opinion/blogs/world-report/articles/2016-02-03/the-pentagon-could-reach-a-historic-level-of-wasteful-spending

3. https://en.wikipedia.org/wiki/Aleksandr_Solzhenitsyn

4. Tolle, Eckhart: *Stillness Speaks,* (New World Library, Novato, CA, 2003), 16

5. http://time.com/3858309/attention-spans-goldfish/

6. https://en.wikipedia.org/wiki/John_Taylor_Gatto

7. Gatto, John Taylor: *Dumbing Us Down*, (New Society Publishers, Gabriola Island, BC Canada, 2005), 61

8. Buhner, Stephen Harrod: *Plant Intelligence and the Imaginal Realm,* (Bear & Company, Rochester, NY, 2014) , 97

9. Lynne McTaggart: *The Field* (Harper Perennial, 2008), 138

10. https://en.wikipedia.org/wiki/Pareto_principle

11. Carroll, Lewis: *Alice in Wonderland* (Bantam Classics, 1984), 167

Chapter Three

1. https://en.wikipedia.org/wiki/Lyall_Watson

2. http://www.infinitebeing.com/0507/monkeys.htm and Key Keyes book

3. http://www.newser.com/story/93224/whales-suffer-like-humans.html

4. http://www.naturalnews.com/
   041736_modern_science_false_assumptions_consciousness.html

5. Ibid 4.

6. http://www.scientificamerican.com/slideshow/achievements-of-
   wandering-minds/

7. http://www.cracked.com/article_20498_5-famous-things-you-wont-
   believe-were-invented-in-dreams.html

8. http://moondoglanding.weebly.com/articles/the-dyl-spud-webb-has-
   springs-for-legs

9. Sisgold, Steve: *What Your Body Is Telling You?* (McGraw Hill, NY,
   2009), 24

10. Buhner, Stephen Harrod: *Plant Intelligence and The Imaginal Realm*
    (Bear & Company, Rochester, NY, 2014), 147

11. http://www.npr.org/sections/13.7/2016/05/04/476717308/after-10-
    years-an-inconvenient-truth-is-still-inconvenient

Chapter Four

1. https://en.wikipedia.org/wiki/Individuation

2. McTaggart, Lynne: *The Field* (Harper Perennial, 2008), 139

3. Eaton, Heather: *The Intellectual Journey of Thomas Berry: Imagining
   the Earth Community*, (Lexington Books, 2014), 232

4. Harvey, Andrew: *The Hope,* (Hay House, Inc., 2009), 147

5. Hill, Napoleon: *Think and Grow Rich* (Napoleon Hill Foundation, 1937), 45

6. Buhner, Stephen Harrod: *Plant Intelligence and The Imaginal Realm,* (Bear & Company, Rochester, NY, 2014), 167

7. http://www.thenation.com/article/good-news-on-climate-changeand-bad-news/

Chapter Five

1. *The Holy Bible*, Genesis 1:26

2. Hill, Napoleon: *Think and Grow Rich,* (Napoleon Hill Foundation, 1937), 45

3. http://www.bbc.com/earth/story/20150706-humans-are-not-unique-or-special

4. http://www.firstpeople.us/FP-Html-Wisdom/ChiefSeattle.html

5. http://www.snre.umich.edu/~dallan/nre220/outline5.htm

6. Kanner, Allen D. Kanner and Gomes, Mary E.: T*he All-Consuming Self*, from *Ecopsychology*, (Sierra Club Books, San Francisco, CA, 1995) 91.

7. Buhner, Stephen Harrod: *Plant Intelligence and the Imaginal Realm,* (Bear & Company, Rochester, NY, 2014), 361

8. http://news.discovery.com/animals/insects/1500-butterfly-species-found-in-single-park-160318.htm

Chapter Six

1. http://www.damanhur.org/en/research-and-experimentation/the-plant-world

2. Buhner, Stephen Harrod: *The Lost Language of Plants,* (Chelsea Green Publishing Company, Vermont, 2002), 7

3. http://www.newser.com/story/177083/how-my-dog-learned-a-toddler-level-vocabulary.html

4. http://www.camilogallardo.com/index.php/therapy/face-to-face

Chapter Seven

1. McTaggart, Lynne: *The Intention Experiment,* (Free Press, NY, 2007), 155

2. http://guymcpherson.com/

3. https://en.wikipedia.org/wiki/
    List_of_scientists_opposing_the_mainstream_scientific_assessment_of
    _global_warming

4. http://www.pbs.org/wgbh/frontline/article/investigation-finds-exxon-
    ignored-its-own-early-climate-change-warnings/

5. http://www.huffingtonpost.com/entry/environmentalists-
    killed-2015_us_57678e8ee4b015db1bc9be9a?section=

6. https://books.google.com/books?
    id=dEerJuhfwIoC&pg=PA109&lpg=PA109&dq=rendered+us+docile,
    +helpless.+If+we+want+to+protest,+it+suppresses+our
    +protest.&source=bl&ots=vw7aCf-6ov&sig=VENvHOJg25Ct4BJZ1ZDLi
    BZyYsE&hl=en&sa=X&ved=0ahUKEwjMk7nYhp7PAhVCkx4KHScNCd
    8Q6AEINDAE#v=onepage&q=rendered%20us%20docile%2C
    %20helpless.%20If%20we%20want%20to%20protest%2C%20it
    %20suppresses%20our%20protest.&f=false

7. https://www.aei.org/publication/18-spectacularly-wrong-apocalyptic-
    predictions-made-around-the-time-of-the-first-earth-day-in-1970-expect-
    more-this-year-3/

8. https://en.wikipedia.org/wiki/Broughton_Suspension_Bridge

9. http://www.historyandheadlines.com/april-12-1831-marching-soldiers-
    cause-suspension-bridge-collapse/

Chapter Eight

1. http://www.scientificamerican.com/article/newborn-babies-chemicals-
    exposure-bpa/

Chapter Nine

6. https://en.wikipedia.org/wiki/Where_no_man_has_gone_before

Chapter Ten

1. Sheldrake, Rupert: *Science Set Free*, (Crown Publishing, Random House, New York, 2012), 156

2. https://en.wikipedia.org/wiki/F._Scott_Fitzgerald

3. Ehrenreich , Barbara: *Bright-Sided*, (Metropolitan Books, NY, 2009), 13

4. http://io9.gizmodo.com/5901172/10-pieces-of-evidence-that-plants-are-smarter-than-you-think

5. https://www.srpl.net/the-law-of-precession/

Chapter Eleven

1. https://en.wikipedia.org/wiki/Intent_(military)

2. http://www.premierbusinesslending.com/business-strategy/business-strategy-commanders-intent/

3. http://www.newser.com/story/77384/scientists-dolphins-are-non-human-persons.html

Chapter Twelve

1. http://mic.com/articles/82483/experience-just-how-much-space-junk-is-floating-around-in-one-astounding-interactive#.9vaMotSHB

2. http://io9.gizmodo.com/5623112/the-smell-of-freshly-cut-grass-is-actually-a-plant-distress-call

3. https://en.wikipedia.org/wiki/1_in_60_rule

Chapter Thirteen

1. http://www.newser.com/story/66456/dogs-as-smart-as-2-year-olds.html

2. https://en.wikipedia.org/wiki/Henry_Ford

3. http://quoteinvestigator.com/2015/02/03/you-can/

Chapter Fourteen

1. https://en.wikipedia.org/wiki/The_Secret_(2006_film)

2. Ibid 1.

3. http://io9.gizmodo.com/5901172/10-pieces-of-evidence-that-plants-are-smarter-than-you-think

4. Ehrenreich, Barbara: *Bright - Sided*, (Metropolitan Books, NY, 2009), 206

Chapter Fifteen

1. http://io9.gizmodo.com/5901172/10-pieces-of-evidence-that-plants-are-smarter-than-you-think

2. *http://aphelis.net/speech-graduates-woody-allen-1979/*

3. Sewall, Laura: *The Skill of Ecological Perception, from Ecopsychology – Restoring the Earth, Healing the Mind,* Edited by Roszak, Theodore, (Sierra Club, 1995), 204

4. Ibid 3., 205

5. Ibid 3., 206

6. Ibid 3., 206

7. Buhner, Stephen Harrod: *Plant Intelligence and The Imaginal Realm,* (Bear & Company, Rochester, NY, 2014), 167

8. Ibid 3., 208

9. https://www.goodreads.com/author/quotes/15332.Rachel_Carson

10. Ibid 3., 210

11. Ibid 3., 213

12. Ibid 3., 214

Chapter Sixteen

1. http://news.discovery.com/animals/top-10-most-intelligent-animals-150325.htm

Chapter Seventeen

1. Jenkinson, Stephen: *Die Wise,* (North Atlantic Books, Berkeley, CA, 2015), 107

2. http://www.newser.com/story/52852/rock-throwing-chimp-proves-he-can-plan.html

Chapter Eighteen

1. Oliver, Mary: *Wild Geese*, from *Eco Therapy – Healing Ourselves, Healing the Earth* by Howard Clinebell, (Augsburg Fortress, Minneapolis, 1996), 188

2. http://io9.gizmodo.com/5901172/10-pieces-of-evidence-that-plants-are-smarter-than-you-think

3. https://www.biblegateway.com/passage/?search=Luke +15%3A11-32&version=ESV

Chapter Nineteen

1. http://io9.gizmodo.com/5901172/10-pieces-of-evidence-that-plants-are-smarter-than-you-think

2. https://www.psychologytoday.com/blog/evil-deeds/201204/essential-secrets-psychotherapy-what-is-the-shadow

3. http://www.goodreads.com/quotes/705426-each-time-a-man-stands-up-for-an-ideal-or

4. Harvey, Andrew: *The Hope,* (Hay House, Inc., 2009), 186

5. https://en.wikipedia.org/wiki/Prayer_of_Saint_Francis

Chapter Twenty

1. Macy, Joanna: quoted in *Eco Therapy – Healing Ourselves, Healing the Earth* by Howard Clinebell, (Augsburg Fortress, Minneapolis, 1996), 65

2. http://www.pri.org/stories/2014-01-09/new-research-plant-intelligence-may-forever-change-how-you-think-about-plants

3. Clinebell, Howard: *Eco Therapy – Healing Ourselves, Healing the Earth,* (Augsburg Fortress, Minneapolis, 1996), 13

4. Walter R. Christie, from *Eco Therapy – Healing Ourselves, Healing the Earth* by Howard Clinebell, (Augsburg Fortress, Minneapolis, 1996) 37

Chapter Twenty-One

1. http://www.rogerebert.com/reviews/great-movie-2001-a-space-odyssey-1968

2. Ibid 1.

3. https://en.wikipedia.org/wiki/List_of_dystopian_films

4. David Bresler, PhD and Martin Rossman, MD: *Academy for Guided Imagery manual,* (Awareness Press, Malibu, 2008),

5. Ibid 4.

6. http://www.pri.org/stories/2014-01-09/new-research-plant-intelligence-may-forever-change-how-you-think-about-plants

7. http://www.rogerebert.com/reodyssey-1968

Chapter Twenty-Two

1. Kingsley, Peter: *Reality,* (Golden Sufi Center, Port Reyes, CA, 2003), 258

2. Harvey, Andrew: *The Hope,* (Hay House, Inc., 2009), 53

3. http://www.newser.com/story/143996/baboon-readers-pick-out-real-words.html

4. Hanh, Thich Nhat: *Love Letter to the Earth,* (Parallax Press, Berkley, CA, 2013), 28

5. Edited by Roszak, Theodore: *The Psychology of Perception, from Ecopsychology – Restoring the Earth, Healing the Mind,* (Sierra Club, 1995), 53

6. http://www.happyplanetindex.org/countries/united-states-of-america/

7. http://www.sapphyr.net/natam/indian.htm

8. http://lifehopeandtruth.com/bible/10-commandments/the-ten-commandments/10-commandments-list/

Chapter Twenty-Three

1. http://www.pri.org/stories/2014-01-09/new-research-plant-intelligence-may-forever-change-how-you-think-about-plants

2. http://trofire.com/2015/07/31/the-worlds-wealthy-are-hiding-up-to-32-trillion-in-offshore-accounts-3/

3. http://money.cnn.com/2015/05/11/technology/overseas-cash-tech/

4. http://ivn.us/2015/03/25/hard-truth-improving-americas-infrastructure-need-spend-money/

5. https://www.michaeljournal.org/articles/politics/item/abraham-lincoln-and-john-f-kennedy

6. ibid

7. http://www.citizensamericaparty.org/happiness.html

8. http://www.themindfulword.org/2013/the-substance-behind-money/

Chapter Twenty-Four

1. https://en.wikipedia.org/wiki/Big_Hairy_Audacious_Goal

2. Rumi, translated by Coleman Barks: *A Year with Rumi,* (Harper One, 2006), 55

3. http://www.alternet.org/economy/5-reasons-rich-are-ruining-economy-hoarding-their-money

Chapter Twenty – Five

1. http://www.mindful.org/jon-kabat-zinn-defining-mindfulness/

Chapter Twenty-Six

1. https://en.wikipedia.org/wiki/Osmosis

2. Gatto, John Taylor: *Weapons of Mass Instruction*, (New Society Publishers, Gabriola Island, BC Canada, 2005), xvi

3. Ibid 3.

4. http://www.pri.org/stories/2014-01-09/new-research-plant-intelligence-may-forever-change-how-you-think-about-plants

5. Ibid 4.

Chapter Twenty-Seven

1.   http://www.dailydot.com/layer8/us-government-information-technology-old-systems-gao-report/

2.   Starr, Mirabai: *God of Love*, (Monkfish Book Publishing Company, NY, 2012), 217

3.   http://www.inc.com/jim-schleckser/how-to-avoid-mission-drift-and-stay-true-to-your-purpose.html

4.   http://www.cbsnews.com/news/why-the-buddy-system-works/

5.   http://www.thefreelibrary.com/Decades+of+deception%3A+secrets+of+lead,+asbestos,+and+tobacco.-a056909661

6.   https://www.google.com/search?q=david+suzuki&oq=david+suzu&aqs=chrome.0.0j69i57j0l4.4037j0j1&sourceid=chrome&ie=UTF-8

Chapter Twenty-Eight

1.   http://thesecondprinciple.com/optimal-learning/naturalistic-intelligence/

2.   Buhner, Stephen Harrod: *Plant Intelligence,* (Bear & Company, Rochester, NY, 2014), 361

3.   Jim Blascovich and Jeremy Bailenson from Infinite Reality (William Morrow Publications, 2012), 63

4.   Master Charles Cannon and Will Wilkinson from A*wakening from the American Dream*, (Waterfront Digital Press, San Diego, CA, 2014), 221

5.   Harvey, Andrew: *The Hope,* (Hay House, Inc., 2009), 37

6.   http://www.nativetimes.com/index.php/life/commentary/5044-the-red-road-is-not-for-sale

7.   Harris, Peter: *Zen Poems* (Everyman's Library, 1999), 30

8.   Meade, Michael: *The Water of Life,* (Green Fire Press, Seattle, WA, 2006), 384

Information:

www.willtwilkinson.com

Made in the USA
San Bernardino, CA
02 June 2018